THEY

DON'T GET IT,

DO THEY?

THEY DON'T GET IT, DO THEY?

Communication in the Workplace — Closing the Gap Between Women and Men

Kathleen Kelley Reardon, PH.D.

Little, Brown and Company

BOSTON   NEW YORK   TORONTO   LONDON

FIRST EDITION

The author is grateful for permission to include the following previously copyrighted material: Excerpt from "How I Did It: Getting the Guys on Your Side" by Annette Miller. Copyright © 1993 by Working Woman, Inc.

Library of Congress Cataloging-in-Publication Data

Reardon, Kathleen Kelley.
  They don't get it, do they? : communication in the workplace — closing the gap between women and men / by Kathleen Kelley Reardon. — 1st ed.
    p. cm.
  ISBN 0-316-73641-4
  1. Sex role in the work environment. 2. Communication in organizations. 3. Communication — Sex differences. 4. Communication in organizations — Case studies. 5. Sex discrimination in employment — Case studies. I. Title.
  HD6060.6.R43 1995
  305.42 — dc20   94-40193

10 9 8 7 6 5 4 3 2 1

MV-NY

Published simultaneously in Canada by Little, Brown & Company (Canada) Limited

Printed in the United States of America

TO MY HUSBAND, CHRIS,
AND MY CHILDREN,
DEVIN, RYAN, AND SHANNON

CONTENTS

PREFACE

PATIENCE AND COMPETENCE have proven insufficient to advance women to the top echelons of traditional business. More than two decades of research and study have convinced me that the problem lies not so much in discrimination (although it is part of the equation) but in the enduring nature of dysfunctional communication patterns and the stereotypes that accompany them.

Some experts blame the power imbalance between the sexes, not sex differences per se, for the way women are treated at work. Others argue that women are to blame because they are too "sensitive." This book does not place blame. Its purpose is to identify the everyday interactions between women and men that, rather than bringing them closer to understanding, actually further separate them from each other.

This book also attempts to help women decide what they can do to close the communication divide with male co-workers: the senior vice president whose lofty title fails to change the communication dynamics that keep her from feeling a sense of solidarity with her peers; the aspiring manager who fears that modeling the behaviors of male managers will alienate her from women and men who expect her to be feminine; the twenty-two-year-old marketing manager who wonders when one of her ideas will be implemented; the fifty-five-year-old vice president of an aerospace firm who still can't get a word in edgewise; the professor, doctor, lawyer, banker, nurse, real estate broker, medical technician, government worker, and a host of others who have gained the education, expertise, and experience but still find themselves disenfranchised by their companies. These women aren't as concerned about polarization, backlash, or victimization as they are about "what to do next." This book attempts to provide some answers.

As a communication and management researcher, I might be inclined to report on the differences between female and male communication and go no further than to suggest further avenues for research. A researcher does not typically advocate ways that women and men might reduce the impact of their differences. Some researchers argue that the pursuit of objective science can become muddled when scientists give advice. But my other roles, those of management professor and business consultant, require me to help people *change*. In this book, therefore, I report what researchers and practitioners have found regarding gender differences, and I also offer advice; not about what you should do, but what you might do based on your personal style and the types of situations you face. Communication is complex. There is always more than one way to achieve any goal, and communication goals are no exception. But we can stretch and even transform ourselves by learning and experimenting with new ways of talking.

Whenever a researcher writes a book, professional questions inevitably arise: What was your sample population? What statistical procedures did you use to analyze your data? Some fields of study do lend themselves readily to quantitative analyses; my own work is largely of that type. But to be valid, quantitative social science research must be informed by direct observation of and interaction with the kinds of people under study. When doing cross-cultural negotiation research I'm regularly reminded that it isn't enough to count how many times a person speaks "directly" in order to know whether such "directness" is prized or despised. The same directness that is prized in the United States can be considered arrogance in Japan. Even within a culture, such differences in interpretation occur. Behaviors that in men would be considered indicative of leadership potential may be seen as crass self-promotion in women.

Research and consulting have provided me many opportunities to learn how gender differences in expectations play out in communication at work. I've also drawn on my collegial interactions at the University of Southern California School of Business and its Leadership Institute and my work with midcareer students in USC's MBA, International MBA (IBEAR), and Executive MBA programs to help understand why women and men in business so often believe of each other: "They don't get it, do they?" This book distills their thoughts and the observations of hundreds of business people and academics. Many names have been disguised because of the fear women have that they might be labeled as feminists or troublemakers. It draws heavily on quantitative studies, but goes beyond observation of systematic differences in male and female talk to reach for understanding of what women and men *think* of these differences, and what they can *do* about them.

Ultimately, this book is about the respect that women richly deserve but all too infrequently find at work. Certainly there are men who long for respect as well, and they will identify with many of the examples in this book. But women as a group — and this includes many at the highest levels of their professions — experience what I refer to as a quicksand of indifference and disregard. After years of studying, toiling, sacrificing, dressing for success, keeping a low profile, attempting to convince men of their competence, the vast majority of women are still underutilized and undervalued at work. There are exceptions, companies where mutual respect is ingrained in the culture. But in most traditional organizations men and women are not speaking the same language. What women say and do doesn't square with images of leadership that were contrived long before women became part of the business landscape.

I chose the title, *They Don't Get It, Do They?*, because it has resonance for women. When I attended the Global Forum for Women in Dublin, Ireland, two years ago, I saw that this phrase had become widely understood by female business and political leaders around the world. Women then said repeatedly and continue to say, "Things were supposed to be better by now." After all, the women's movement forged and paved the path. Talented women entered the workplace expecting someday to be welcome. But the women I've studied, observed, and worked with know that this is not the case. The communication divide between women and men at work takes its daily toll.

If laws and diversity programs aren't sufficient to change the day-to-day interactions of men and women at work, we must rely on what we can trust: the initiative of individuals. This book is about individual women becoming change agents. It is about women expanding their communication skills to facilitate their own advancement and that of other women. It's about women and men seeing how their communication habits contribute to the dearth of women at senior management levels.

Business success for women requires getting beyond the common fear of being labeled "feminist" or "troublemaker" to a position of self-respect and confidence. This can be achieved only if individual women and men break down old ways of thinking, find common ground in the midst of differences, and begin talking about options for mutual gain. History has taught us that when it comes to building bridges between the genders, progress is both hard-won and often superficial. Waiting for large organizations to "get it" is a waste of precious time and talent. Individuals, however, can help close the communication gap between women and men at work. Many already do so daily. This book was written for and about them. Enlightenment, after all, often comes one candle at a time.

ACKNOWLEDGMENTS

THIS BOOK WOULD not have been possible without the encouragement and assistance of many people. First among them are my mother and father. To them my being born a girl was as wonderful as if I were a boy. To them there was as much reason for a girl to achieve as a boy. They taught this to me in direct and indirect ways. They taught it to my brother, Kevin, whose own years of success in the Navy did not lead to gender favoritism by him or my sister-in-law, Susan, either. Both their son, Brian, and daughter, Meghan, are currently midshipmen at the Naval Academy. There are few things so valuable as parents who believe that you can succeed no matter your gender.

I wish my father had lived to read this book. He was a constant inspiration in my work even when he wasn't sure why I had chosen to study communication instead of chemistry. My mother is still living and I want to take this opportunity to say that those mornings when she awoke, scraped ice off the car window, rushed off to work, and still at the end of a long day had time to be the PTA president and a heck of a Girl Scout leader were an inspiration. My parents were not perfect. I don't know any who are. They were, however, two people who within their means assured that their children, male and female, were given the best education an absence of money could buy.

My appreciation is also extended to my husband, Chris, who, using his words, is "at least 93 percent feminist." To him "feminist" does not describe closed-minded, antimen sentiments. It describes equal treatment for men and women. With two careers we struggle at times to do all that is needed at work and home. There are days when it seems impossible to meet all the deadlines and demands. But we manage to support each other's endeavors and give our children the love and support they richly deserve. Chris is my best editor and harshest critic, next to myself, and he even occasionally exceeds me. Yet it is this criticism that encourages me, and it is balanced by his continued support.

I have also been fortunate to work with a number of wonderful people. Warren Bennis, guru of leadership, is my mentor and friend. I have learned much from Warren. When he asked me to be a director in the Leadership Institute he founded at the University of Southern California, I did not realize the many lessons that awaited me and the value I'd derive working with him and the Presidential Fellows on a regular basis. He also brought into my life one of his friends, a woman who had inspired me long before I met her. Betty Friedan has been a Distinguished Visiting Professor of Business and Leadership at USC for three years. Betty is my friend. She is a never-ending source of knowledge. Thirty years my senior, she is in so many ways my age or younger. Her vitality and passion for the issues that confront women have been a constant inspiration. Rarely showing a soft side to the public, she has shown it to me. Her desire for me to achieve and her faith in my ability, even when she and I disagree, have made a lasting impression.

Two other female colleagues to whom I am indebted are Jon Goodman, director of the USC Entrepreneur Program, from whom I draw strength and perspective and share great humor, and Gail Fairhurst, chair of Communication at the University of Cincinnati, and a constant friend. My thanks to Alan Rowe and Burt Nanus, who read and commented on the leadership chapter. There are a host of others, faculty and students, in the International MBA (IBEAR), Executive MBA, and MBA programs who shared with me their ideas and experiences.

Ph.D. students Vicki Whiting and Emmeline dePillis helped with my research. Marcia Knous, Administrative Coordinator at the Leadership Institute, and Dan Rodrigues, work study, helped get the final manuscript in shape. Joan Worden was my able assistant with references. Niloo Norouzi was a great help in gathering research. My appreciation also goes to the hundreds of women and men who answered my endless questions and who provided the experiences and examples in this book.

My thanks also to my friends who are a constant support, especially Ellen Nichols, Marianne Tegner, Richard Lewis, Barry and Beth Simon, Mark and Susan Harris, Shelley Taylor, Tom and Lois Valliere, and Aminta Tamayo. My sincere appreciation to my extended family and the encouragement I receive from Connie and Earl Noblet.

To my agent, Peter Ginsberg, my very deep appreciation for his constant support, invaluable guidance, and encouragement. And to Fredi Friedman, my editor at Little, Brown, who wanted to publish this book and wouldn't let it be less than she envisioned, my gratitude. Thanks also to Janice Pomerance, Becky Michaels, and Peggy Freudenthal at Little, Brown and to copyeditor Faith Hanson. Special thanks to Sara McCune, my first editor from Sage Publications, who trusted me to write a book despite my then tender age and continues to support me in all my literary efforts.

Finally, my children deserve appreciation. Too young to know why mom likes to spend so much time putting words into a machine that seems to make so many errors, they nevertheless occasionally let me work. Stopping by to get splinters removed, to take learning-to-read pauses, or just to talk was as much a part of this book as the research behind it. I finished many a page after 9 P.M. listening to them chatter with each other in their room, resisting sleep to the last possible minute.

THEY

DON'T GET IT,

DO THEY?

‖ 1 ‖

THE COMMUNICATION CHALLENGE

IN THE SPRING of 1993, a group of fifty business leaders gathered at the Loews resort hotel on the ocean cliffs of Santa Monica, California. They were there to discuss a problem that will not go away: Far too few women are making it to the top of traditional organizations.

Since 1982 women have earned more than half of all bachelor degrees. By 1985 women were earning 45 percent of the degrees in business. Their share of MBA degrees increased from 8 percent in 1975 to 31 percent in 1985. Today, of the total number of managerial/professional employees, 44 percent are women. Yet study after study reports that in large companies less than 5 percent of senior managers are women.

At the Santa Monica meeting, the mostly female group wrestled with the question What is holding women back? Some women blamed themselves; some blamed men, but most left the meeting as puzzled as when they arrived. Diversity programs were spreading like wildfire, and male senior executives were telling their employees to learn tolerance. Yet these women managers wondered: What happened to the expected promotions? What happened to the idea that if we can just get in the door and prove ourselves the rest will be a piece of cake? Critical mass was supposed to force open the executive suite doors to women. Wasn't 44 percent a critical mass?

The discussion turned heated at times. Frustration surfaced. The women spoke of their growing impatience with the rigidity of American corporations, their distrust of diversity programs serving as a cover for biases against women, and the erosion of women's value at work. They blamed these conditions for the exodus of middle- and senior-level women who were joining the ranks of entrepreneurs. Women-owned businesses grew 35 percent from 1989 to 1990. Forty to 50 percent of all businesses in the year 2000 may well be owned by women. Many are skipping the trials and tribulations, the injustices and biases of the fast track of traditional organizations that have proven less than fast for them. They are starting their own companies, where they can start at the top.

For every woman who leaves a traditional organization to start a business, however, far more remain behind. They are the women for whom this book was written. These women are tired of playing the game well and losing. They've dressed for success, earned the right academic degrees, postponed or decided against parenthood, studiously avoided behaviors that might be construed as feminist or feminine, taken on tough assignments, and learned the lingo. The payoffs have paled by comparison to the trade-offs.

Most women no longer believe that the only obstacle to their success is the "glass ceiling." They don't get high enough to catch a glimpse of it. Their energies are focused on fighting the disturbing, sinking sensation that something is swallowing their ankles and pulling at their knees — a relentless quicksand of indifference and disregard. It manifests itself in meetings where women speak and are not heard. It is demonstrated by male-only informal meetings over golf or racquetball. It is composed of slights and oversights, special criteria for advancement not imposed on men, and a host of misinterpretations of female behaviors based on outmoded stereotypes.

For women who have cracked the glass ceiling, the story is much the same. They knock themselves out getting near the top only to discover that it's just more of the same — long hours of proving yourself. And the proving never stops. In most cases, no amount of competence counteracts this trend, especially now that women are competing with men for "their jobs."[1]

Shirley Peterson, vice president of business practices at Northrop Corporation, agrees. "For women, it's more than lonely at the top," she told me. "You're usually one of one or two women present at any meeting. You're highly visible. But this doesn't mean you are making an impact. It's very easy for them to ignore what you have to say. You have to be willing to speak up and occasionally make a fuss or they won't pay attention to you."

If these were the sentiments of only a few women, they could perhaps be dismissed. But female traders, marketers, advertisers, salespeople, finance executives, lawyers, and doctors share the same perceptions. They have found, with few exceptions, that the barriers to entry keep changing. Behind each door they wrench open, they find another. Their pay has been less than that of their male colleagues and the hours have gotten longer and longer. Despite efforts to be noticed for their individual competencies, talented women are recognizing they have something in common: They are not reaching senior levels in numbers large enough to make a difference for themselves or those women who follow them.

WHAT IS THE PROBLEM?

The most obvious explanation is discrimination. Surely it is part of the equation. It rears its ugly head in inequitable pay structures, tardy promotions, and sexual harassment. But discrimination, loathsome as it is, isn't the major problem. Alone, it would not have kept so many determined women from achieving their career goals. Critical mass would have helped women work their way into 15 to 20 percent of senior executive suites by now.

The women I meet in organizations across the United States and those I teach in MBA and Executive MBA classes know there is a less conspicuous enemy that plagues women of considerable competence. Even in companies known for their antidiscrimination policies, women are confronted by this quiet enemy. They are coming to realize that the greatest obstacle to their advancement is not among the frequently touted list, including the glass ceiling, sexism, unhelpful husbands, or the absence of team sports experience. It is something less tangible, more deniable than overt discrimination.

At the heart of the problem is the fact that men and women working together do not speak the same language. It is easy to be deceived when both speak fluently a language such as English. The words are similar, but the selection and impact are far different for men than they are for women. The verbal and nonverbal languages men use at work are frequently different from those used by women. And despite years of trying, few women have become truly fluent in worksite male-speak.

Fundamental differences in the way women and men think as described by Carol Gilligan in her book *A Different Voice* lead to fundamental differences in the way they communicate job commitment, managerial expertise, leadership, and a host of other promotion-related competencies.[2] For too long business academics and practitioners have been hesitant to acknowledge that men and women experience life, and therefore work as well, in different ways. We worry about saying that men and women differ. But they do, if not innately, then because of socialization; and the way they communicate these experiences is therefore different as well.

In research studies far too numerous to mention, sex roles have proven a significant determinant of human behavior. As Gilligan points out, since it is difficult to say "different" without saying "better" or "worse" — and since the usual standards of measurement developed by men favor male styles of behavior — when women's behaviors do not conform, the conclusion is that something is wrong with women.

Even when women act in ways perfectly acceptable for men, the interpretations are different. One of my male colleagues, knowing of my intention to write this book, said, "Don't forget to include femi-Nazis in there too." He explained that he had just returned from a presentation by a CEO who is invited to speak on the campus each year. After the speech, the CEO had shown a video to the group after which a woman had stood up and said, "Where I work we wouldn't use that video. There isn't enough minority representation in it." My colleague said to me, "Now that's a femiNazi. She just challenged him in front of everyone. And the video did have some minorities and women in it."

I asked my colleague if perhaps there was more to the story. "After all," I said, "men around here challenge visiting speakers on a regular basis." I asked, "Was she abrupt or rude?" "No," he said, "it was just an unnecessary comment and it wasn't accurate." I pressed further:

"So a femiNazi is a woman who speaks out in a way that seems inaccurate?" He said, "She just didn't know what she was talking about. I'm just learning about femiNazis myself, but she seems like one to me."

Expectations regarding communication at work have been developed by men, for men. Thus, women are often seen as displaying too much or too little of a male-preferred form of behavior. They may be labeled too demure, too controlling, too concerned about feelings, not adequately focused on tasks, or ill at ease with getting rid of the "deadwood" among employees. Each conclusion is based on standards that deny the value of women's ways of thinking and communicating.

Women's standards of professional behavior are frequently out of sync with those of male colleagues. An example of this mismatch of standards is found in women's perceptions of boasting. A female senior vice president asked me, "Don't men know what women are thinking when they posture, position, and play the my-dog-is-better-than-your-dog game? It's hard to watch." The answer to her question is that much of the time neither sex knows what the other is thinking.

Communication researchers Lynn Miller, Linda Cooke, Jennifer Tsang, and Faith Morgan studied boasting behavior and found that men and women interpret self-promotion quite differently.[3] Female boasts tend to be understated compared to those of men. Men's boasts "are more extreme and less like 'positive statements' than those of women." Men make greater use of superlatives involving social comparison or competition; women tend to make positive statements about how well things went or how much effort was expended. Women are generally more hesitant to emphasize that they are the best or better than others.

Miller and her colleagues found that the female approach elicits greater liking and praise for social sensitivity, but male boasting creates the impression that the boaster is competent, confident, proud, and successful.

In a conversation with a former university program director, I asked if he was willing to consider changing his mind on an important matter. He turned to his right, pointed to a male colleague seated beside him, and said, "You ask Bill here. He'll tell you I'm one of the most open-minded guys you'll ever meet. Isn't that right, Bill?" Even a few minutes of conversation with this man reveals immediately that he is far from open-minded, but he boasted without restraint about his competence in this area. To me and a female colleague seated next to me, it sounded rather silly. To him, evidently, it was all part of a regular day of talking about himself with confidence.

All men do not go about boasting, but most do know how to let it be known that they are awfully good at something important. They can make the mundane sound important and their role seem pivotal. For a woman to boast like a man, she must act in ways counter to her socialization. Women who accomplish this usually find that men are uncomfortable with boastful women. So boasting like a man often brings women no greater reward than not boasting at all. Women are left to prove themselves without promoting themselves in environments where skillful self-promotion often brings impressive rewards.

Law firms are a good example. U.S. Bankruptcy Judge Lisa Hill Fenning has observed women failing to advance their own reputations by refraining from boasting. "Women lawyers aren't trained to tell their own war stories," she told me. "They tend not to leave the courtroom and tell the first five people they see about the case they just won. Men engage in ways of telling their stories without seeming to boast, like using self-deprecating humor as they report back from the battlefront. Women who make it in law firms learn to communicate their successes rather than merely go back to their desks to pick up the next piece of paper."

Speaking with Lorna Hennington, a recent law school graduate, I heard the same story. "Men tell you what they've done," she said. "They say something like, 'Let me tell you what happened in court today. I didn't get everything I wanted but, wow!' Then they go on with the story."

Based on eleven years of practice before taking the bench Judge Fenning noted that women have to be able to say, "You won't believe what happened in court today" followed by a description of the challenge they faced and how they overcame it. This takes some practice, and it can be initially uncomfortable for women who are more accustomed to listening to men's war stories than telling their own. But leaving your accomplishments to their imagination is not productive.

UNDERESTIMATING THE MAGNITUDE OF THE TASK

When traveling on airplanes, I occasionally converse with the person seated next to me. Several times women have asked me, "What do you do for a living?" I respond, "I'm a business professor. I teach persuasion and negotiation." Some leave their seats shortly thereafter to walk down the aisle, no doubt thinking that if they stay I might sell them something before the plane lands. Others ask, "Can you teach me a few persuasion and negotiation techniques to use with men? I could really use them at work." I do know some techniques, but this request belies a perspective on communication that has led women down the wrong path for years. We treat a very complex form of human interaction as something that can be mastered with a few lessons about male modes of communication.

Women derived significant benefits from the lessons in Betty Lehan Harragan's *Games Mother Never Taught You*[4] and Margaret Hennig and Anne Jardim's *The Managerial Woman*.[5] These books, published in 1977 and 1976, respectively, launched a paradigm shift in female thinking. They, and other such writings, encouraged women to acquire political savvy, learn the ropes, and beat men at their own games. There is much to be said for political savvy and learning the ropes, but it gets you only so far — approximately as far as women have gotten.

Years later, businesswomen are choosing one of two philosophies or alternating between them. The first is a sort of knock-'em sock-'em approach in which women attempt to outsmart men at their own game. This has its roots in *Games Mother Never Taught You* and books of its type. The second is the cooperative-and-competent approach: Keep your head low, do your job, and they can't stop you. The latter is common wisdom passed mostly from senior men to junior women. It is good advice, but not good enough to get women to the top. Despite women's competence, "they" could stop women, and in most cases "they" did.

These two philosophies have something significant in common: They are too simplistic given the complexity of the task. In the first case, men do not like anyone beating them at their games, let alone a newcomer and, worse, a woman. In the second case, women have said for years that they have to be twice as good as men to be considered competent. Even then, many men are programmed by their work culture not to notice.

Shelley Taylor, a UCLA psychology professor and author of *Positive Illusions,* believes that these male responses apply especially when women are near or in senior positions. "The cute-and-little effect doesn't apply then," Taylor told me. "When women are no longer cute-and-little, they are threatening. Men aren't as accepting of them. They've never learned to comfortably accommodate female peers, especially ones who might disagree with them or even tell them what to do." Young women who go merrily along thinking there isn't any problem between women and men, that the feminists are making it all up, find one day not long after a promotion that the same men who seemed perfectly content with them as "cute-and-little" subordinates are now critical and unhelpful.

Women are generally unprepared to deal with such precipitous declines in collegial support. Often they wonder what they've done wrong. As Taylor sees it, "The whole process of learning that men really aren't all that comfortable with women at senior levels is very painful for women."

Many men do fervently wish for women to be treated as equals. But most draw the line where it might affect them personally. A CEO recently shared with me his private opinion on the matter of women's equality. "I have to tell you, in all honesty, men are getting quieter and quieter," he said. "There's something very damaging going on. I believe there is a backlash. It's not a conspiracy, but a growing antagonism that manifests itself in fewer opportunities for women. It's rooted in feelings a lot of men have but don't admit to. I'll give you an example. A few years back, I belonged to an all-male club. In time it became *the* club to belong to if you wanted to get ahead. We decided to vote on whether to let women join. I was in favor because the club gave its members a business advantage. But, to be honest, when women began to join, I felt sort of invaded. Maybe that's not the best word, but I felt that something had been taken away. I had enjoyed the exclusively male camaraderie. These women had taken that. I didn't want to feel that way, but I did. You know, I think I'm pretty sensitive to women wanting to get ahead. So what must other men be feeling? It makes you wonder, doesn't it?"

Women have underestimated the magnitude of the communication differences between women and men as well as the willingness of men to change the landscape of the workplace. The idea that men would let women into the game and accept them as equal players has proven false, especially at senior levels. Few men will admit it in public, but stories like the one above have leaked out over and over in the course of my interviews with men. Research by business professors O. C. Brenner, Joseph Tomkiewicz, and Virginia Schein confirms that not much has changed in this regard in over fifteen years. They explain:

> The attitudes of male managers, the predominant decision makers at upper levels, have not changed, and those attitudes may well be negatively affecting women's opportunities to advance into positions of power and influence. If not, affirmative action and fear of lawsuits will provide opportunities for women up to the middle ranks, but the strongly held attitude of "think manager — think male" among decision makers who are men will keep women confined to middle-level jobs.[6]

The idea of having to file lawsuits in order to get ahead is generally distasteful to women. Common wisdom suggests it is career suicide. "Everyone knows that you're a marked woman once you sue," a leading female business professor explains. "The word gets out. And women fear they won't get a job anywhere else."

What About the Younger Men?

Given the intransigence of the present generation of male senior executives, many women look to the next generation. Will it be different when younger men come into power? they wonder. Ask nearly any young woman getting an MBA in a leading business school whether she thinks this is true. Ask any female manager who has drawn new hires from this crop. Most doubt it. As one female Executive MBA student said to me, "The cases we study are almost all selected by male professors. We hardly ever see a female professor. The jokes are male, the philosophies are male. The books are written by men. Not much has changed."

Business Week described this phenomenon in an article entitled "Where Are All the Female B-School Profs?" Few of the leading business schools escape unscathed in discussions of female faculty promotions. Only 8 percent of the tenured faculty of the top twenty schools are female. As *Business Week* suggested, there appears to be "a glass ceiling in the ivory tower."[7]

Young or old, businessmen have been given little incentive to learn how women think or to patiently study female communication patterns. Look at it from their perspective. Women are a relatively new element in an environment where accommodating novelty is talked about more often than it happens. What payoffs accrue from understanding women at work? Tolerating them is one thing. Laws require that. But making efforts to understand them is something else entirely.

With the situation so unpromising, women are becoming more vocal. Men, even many of the sympathetic ones, are also getting tired of being blamed for what they see as vague attacks by women. Most see themselves as innocent bystanders in a system not sensitive to them either. As one forty-four-year-old male public relations executive complained, "If I hear one more attack on white males, I'm going to explode. All of a sudden I'm the enemy. Nothing I say seems to change that. I'm lumped in with a whole bunch of other guys I don't even like. If women want me to be sensitive to their issues, they'll have to stop blaming me for the whole problem. I take my share of responsibility, but they have some too. If they want me to see them as individuals, I'd like the same courtesy."

Some experts argue that the relationship between men and women at work is strained to the breaking point. There are those who believe women are creating a "sexual separation." Support for this view can be found in the popular press. In a 1994 *Newsweek* article, Diana Trilling argues that women have failed to distinguish between sexual nuisance and harassment. The result, she writes, is a "feminist culture which appears to be bent upon raising always-new and higher barriers between men and women." While Trilling recognizes that "there are many forms of male behavior which legitimately call for censure and even for the intervention of law," she advises that feminists "take warning from all the other separations which now divide our world" and avoid fostering the idea that men are ruthless aggressors against women.[8]

As in any good argument, there is always some truth to each side. Surely there are women who react strongly to what they see as offensive behavior without considering how they might work with the offender to change things for the better. But my research indicates that there are far more women who have declined to speak up at all. They've tolerated offensive remarks and behaviors because, until recently, they've feared retaliation for doing otherwise. In school and at work, they've been given little training to assist them in responding to the indifference and disregard they experience on a daily basis on the job. Is it any wonder that some lash out? Would things be better if they remained silent just to avoid having to deal with some people who speak up without good cause? The women I've met while writing this book concur that it's time to change things for the better.

A Glimpse at the Future

Megatrends for Women, a 1992 research-based book by Patricia Aburdene and John Naisbitt, is encouraging in its predictions about women's future at work. Finance, they propose, is one of the best places for women. "Even an unreconstructed good old boy is a sucker for sound financial results," they explain. More than half of U.S. accountants are women. The authors' description of finance as a fast track to top management for women may be sound. Their view that high-tech firms offer promise seems reasonable, despite the fact that women hold only 5 percent of vice president and higher positions at the 29,000 high-tech firms studied. After all, the Bureau of Labor Statistics reports that the wage gap for women computer scientists — at 89 percent of what male counterparts earn — is the narrowest of the well-paying jobs.[9]

Clearly, however, this is one of those is-the-glass-half-empty-or-half-full tests. Certainly women are succeeding in many fields. For example, Aburdene and Naisbitt mention that women attorneys are "bringing home big bucks." Law is the best-paying career for women. Yet women are leaving law in large numbers. Laura Mansnerus's April 1993 *Working Woman* article, "Why Women Are Leaving the Law," indicates that the communication climate at law firms is the major culprit. When women lawyers are asked to describe this climate, "one after another mentions the poses, both dominant and submissive, the false socializing, the tantrums, the fraternity-style shows of dedication."[10]

Statistics regarding the future for women at work are worth knowing, but they do not reveal the inside stories. Today women are leaving even high-paying jobs because they are tired of dealing with a communication climate that diminishes the value of all they've worked to achieve. One vice president of a computer products company for which I'd been consulting told me that women leave that company because "we let them go just so far and then no farther. They just have to look around to see that none of them are at my level and likely they won't be in the near future either." He didn't think anyone was consciously keeping women out of the senior ranks, and certainly the company had made some effort to promote women, but the men running the organization couldn't get past their biases regarding women in leadership positions.

A similar story came from an aerospace senior manager who told me that his boss, a woman, is outstanding. But he also shared with me the difficulty she is having with her boss, who sees her as a threat and can't get used to the idea of a woman being promoted to his level.

Downsizing is exacerbating the problem. Specialties where women have tended to congregate are early targets. If men don't "get it" with regard to the value of these women, then letting them go makes sense to them. In the back rooms and boardrooms where bottom-line decisions are being made, the discomfort with women is taking its toll. For women who want a piece of the pie in larger organizations, things are getting worse, not better.

Less than a decade ago, it seemed that improvement was in the offing. Women's efforts were beginning to have an impact. Creating a diverse workforce was becoming a serious undertaking. With female new entrants to the workforce expected to grow to two-thirds between 1987 and 2000, companies wanting to compete and attract the most skilled females were adopting new policies and training their managers to understand how women think.

Then the economy took a downturn. Companies downsized. They

focused on becoming lean and mean. What most companies have now is a significant number of women concentrated at middle and lower levels. The criteria for advancement have become extremely stringent. Everyone is watched. Any single behavior not befitting a potential leader can be grounds for delayed advancement. This is true for both men and women. But women face a greater challenge. The way they communicate often creates the mistaken impression that they are not leader material. Take, for example, an October 1993 *Wall Street Journal* report of AT&T's new expanded assessment process for senior executive hires. Applicants are asked to give brief presentations to an assessment counselor or lead a mock meeting. The simulations help determine a candidate's "cultural background, teaming capability and leadership skills," according to Hal Burlingame, an AT&T vice president. Psychological testing, which had been becoming passé, is making a comeback. Some job candidates are asked to act out roles and endure days of rigorous screening. All this activity is intended to weed out misfits.[11]

Such efforts to find the best fit in new hires may seem harmless. In actuality, they have the potential of weeding out women. Now the absence of diversity at senior levels is once again getting the blessing of senior management. Justified by economic conditions, intolerance of difference is becoming routine at senior levels. The belief that tests and role playing can separate desirable from undesirable candidates is itself strong evidence that there are preferred ways to lead, manage, make decisions, and follow. That these preferred ways are male-defined is of little doubt. The *Wall Street Journal* cited the experience of Joseph Edwards, a candidate for a $300,000-a-year chief financial officer position at an aerospace firm. When he arrived at the interview, fifty other candidates were there as well. He complained about the unprofessional treatment, so the company executives advanced him to the next round of interviews because they liked his outspoken manner.[12]

How long would a woman who has taught herself not to make waves last in a situation like this? Not long. According to an article in *The Economist*, "Made to choose between being thought pushy and being actually self-effacing, women tend to choose the latter. Within mixed groups, even highly qualified women put their views less forcefully than men, and listen much more than they talk."[13]

The Challenge of Change

Halting the exodus of competent women from traditional male-dominated organizations and revising the communication climates of these companies to accommodate women is a tremendous task. Leaving it to senior executives trained in the typical "business-as-usual" or the equally myopic "at any cost cut expenses" schools of organizational design is not likely to prove effective. Such organizations are too busy looking at the short-term bottom line or in rearview mirrors to be open to women.

Rosabeth Moss Kanter, a Harvard Business School professor and author of *The Change Masters,* describes most organizations as having "a preference for being guided by the past rather than the future, by what is already known rather than what is not yet known."[14] Reward systems in such companies are what Kanter terms "payoff-centered" rather than "investment centered." She explains:

> This idea is captured nicely by the "Peter Principle" of promoting a person to his/her level of incompetence. The promotion is a reward for doing the last job, not a bet on capacity for doing the next one. The bonus is available to take home after the results are in, not a pool of funds to use to get results in the first place.[15]

Kanter argues that innovative companies must be more investment-oriented, more future-oriented. People should be promoted before they are ready, so that they stretch to do the next job. The implications for female advancement are clear. Women are an innovation. They are new to the organization and not yet fully tested. Rather than let them stretch to meet the next challenge, women are expected to prove themselves again and again so that change-averse companies can be sure that they are past ready for promotion.[16]

From lack of trying, most traditional male-dominated companies have developed an incapacity to change in order to accommodate women. They don't get it because they haven't had to, and they have little inclination to start now. Men have long held the power both at home and at work. They were raised to be in charge, to accept authority because one day it would be theirs, to play rough because that's life, and to "play along to get along" because that's been the name of the game. "Nine to five" has given way to "seven to seven." Everyone is working harder, not smarter. Raised to compete, many men at the top of organizations have gotten carried away with the fear of competition and worship of the bottom line. Those running the majority of American businesses measure themselves and their subordinates on commitment to work. They're working themselves into early graves and taking some good people with them.

Women have felt the pressure and the fear. Jenifer Morrissey left her position as an engineer with a leading high-tech firm because she was tired of trying to be someone other than herself. "I was afraid to network with women," she told me. "It was clear to me that if a man saw me talking with another woman he would assume that we weren't talking about work, that we were wasting our time. Men don't talk about work all the time. But for women the appearance of not being committed to the job is easily created. Men also wonder whether you're scheming, hatching some plot against them. One time a rare event occurred. Five of the women in marketing happened to be walking down a hallway at the same time. We stopped to talk. A man walked by. He paused and looked over at us. I watched as his eyes moved from one woman to another and finally rested on me. I was terrified. Since then I've learned that many other women harbor the same fear. It's a shame."

According to Rosabeth Moss Kanter, "The threat of change arouses anxiety when it is still just a threat and not an actuality, while too many possibilities are still open, and before people can experience themselves in the new state."[17] Women have not reached high levels of organizations in sufficient numbers to become nonthreatening. They are still an enigma. They are still a source of threat.

But the worst part is not men's fears. Those are natural during the course of change. When women, even senior women, are afraid to be themselves, to communicate even occasionally in ways natural to their socialization because they fear making men fearful of them, the situation is dire. When they spend more energy dodging labels than doing what they do well, it's time to ask why.

If there is going to be change, it has to start with women. Hoping that men will change or that young ones will "get it" on their own is a waste of time. Proving oneself isn't enough either. Women tried that.

It's time to stop thinking, "If I keep my eye on the ball and hit a home run, they'll have to listen to me." History doesn't bear this out. Research doesn't either. Researchers have identified a frightening phenomenon resulting from too few positive results for women who keep their eye on the ball and do their best. They found that women who give it their all and get little in return often cease to acquire salary-relevant attributes. They give up. This "feedback effect" that discourages women from developing their skills is a sort of catch-22. Women stop trying to prove themselves, thereby reinforcing the stereotypes that inhibited their progress in the first place.[18]

For Women Who Want to Stay

In 1993 after meeting with hundreds of women and listening to their expressions of frustration at finding over and over that men don't get it, I wrote a case based on their experiences that was published in the *Harvard Business Review.* Entitled "The Memo in Every Woman's Desk," the case focused on Elizabeth Ames, who decided to speak up — to risk the labels. She wrote a memo to the CEO of her company. Unlike most women I've interviewed who have written such memos but declined to send them, Liz decided it was time to try to make a difference. Her hope was that the CEO would read her memo and take steps to improve the plight of women in her company, Vision Software. The memo read as follows:

> TO: Mr. John Clark, CEO
> FROM: Elizabeth C. Ames, Director of Consumer Marketing
> DATE: March 8, 1993
>
> I've been working in the marketing department at Vision Software for more than ten years, where I've had my share of challenges and successes. I've enjoyed being part of an interesting and exciting company. Despite my general enthusiasm about the company and my job, however, I was taken aback when I received your memo announcing the resignations of Miriam Blackwell and Susan French, Vision's two most senior women. This is not the first time Vision has lost its highest-ranking women. Just nine months ago, Kathryn Hobbs resigned, and a year before that, it was Susanne

LaHaise. The reasons are surprisingly similar: they wanted to "spend more time with their families" or "explore new career directions."

I can't help but detect a disturbing pattern. Why do such capable, conscientious women who have demonstrated intense commitment to their careers suddenly want to change course or spend more time at home? It's a question I've thought long and hard about.

Despite Vision's policies to hire and promote women and your own efforts to recognize and reward women's contributions, the overall atmosphere in this company is one that slowly erodes a woman's sense of worth and place. I believe that top-level women are leaving Vision Software not because they are drawn to other pursuits but because they are tired of struggling against a climate of female failure. Little things that happen daily — things many men don't even notice and women can't help but notice — send subtle messages that women are less important, less talented, less likely to make a difference than their male peers.

Let me try to describe what I mean. I'll start with meetings, which are a way of life at Vision and one of the most devaluing experiences for women. Women are often talked over and interrupted; their ideas never seem to be heard. Last week, I attended a meeting with ten men and one other woman. As soon as the woman started her presentation, several side conversations began. Her presentation skills were excellent, but she couldn't seem to get people's attention. When it was time to take questions, one man said dismissively, "We did something like this a couple of years ago, and it didn't work." She explained how her ideas differed, but the explanation fell on deaf ears. When I tried to give her support by expressing interest, I was interrupted.

But it's not just meetings. There are many things that make women feel unwelcome or unimportant. One department holds its biannual retreats at a country club with a "men only" bar. At the end of the sessions, the men typically hang around at the bar and talk, while the women quietly disappear. Needless to say, important information is often shared during those casual conversations.

Almost every formal meeting is followed by a series of informal ones behind closed doors. Women are rarely invited. Nor are they privy to the discussions before the formal meetings. As a result, they are often less likely to know what the boss has on his mind and therefore less prepared to react.

My female colleagues and I are also subjected to a daily barrage of seemingly innocent comments that belittle women. A co-worker of mine recently boasted about how much he respects women, saying, "My wife is the wind beneath my wings. In fact, some people call me Mr. Karen Snyder." The men chuckled; the women didn't. And just last week, a male colleague stood up at 5:30 and jokingly informed a group of us that he would be leaving early: "I have to play mom tonight." Women play mom every night, and it never gets a laugh. In fact, most women try to appear devoid of concern about their families.

Any one of these incidents on its own is a small thing. But together and in repetition, they are quite powerful. The women at Vision fight to get their ideas heard and to crack the informal channels of information. Their energy goes into keeping up, not getting ahead, until they just don't have any more to give.

I can assure you that my observations are shared by many women in the company. I can only speculate that they were shared by Miriam Blackwell and Susan French.

Vision needs men and women if it is to become the preeminent educational software company. We need to send stronger, clearer signals that men are not the only people who matter. And this kind of change can work only if it starts with strong commitment at the top. That's why I'm writing to you. If I can be of help, please let me know.[19]

Would you send this memo? Experts, readers of the *HBR* and the *Washington Post*, which carried it on the front page of the Sunday, March 27, 1993, business section, and those who listened to it read on National Public Radio varied in their reactions. Liz supporters argued that women should be able to share with senior management the reasons why their careers are so frequently derailed. Many saw the memo as a sincere attempt to open avenues of communication and to bring about positive change. Those opposed to Liz sending the memo were concerned that the CEO would be unresponsive or, worse, retaliatory. Others argued that going it alone is not safe in business nor effective in bringing about change.

One of the experts responding to the case was Gloria Steinem, author, feminist, and organizer and founder of *Ms.* magazine. An excerpt from her comments was part of my article: "Unless Liz is in imminent danger of hunger or homelessness, I would advise her to send the memo. If she doesn't she is not only acting against her own and other women's long-term interest but also failing to give her company her best advice."[20] Philip A. Marineau, then executive vice president and chief operating officer at the Quaker Oats Company, concurred: "My advice is to send the memo. Sure, it's a risk. But not sending it will lead only to greater frustration — and eventually Liz will resign anyway. Chances are the CEO is already alarmed about the loss of his top two women executives and is wondering what he can do to prevent others from leaving. If he's smart, he'll not only listen to Liz's concerns but also make her a part of the search for solutions."[21] This was also the general perspective of author/businessman Paul Hawkins. In his response he posed the question "How is it that we have created institutions in which people are afraid to express the truth as they see it? Bhopal, Three Mile Island, and the Ford Pinto all were preceded by memos unsent or unread." He also proposed that Liz send the memo: "If she doesn't file the memo, Liz will be left with the new dilemma of subordinating her own wisdom and sense of self to a system that is not fully functional. She will have an aborted sense of her own value, an acute loss in a world that is crying out for more value to be added to it. If business is about adding value, then what better place to find it than within ourselves."[22]

Other experts disagreed. Richard D. Glovsky, former chief of the Civil Division of the United States Attorney's Office in Boston and founder of Glovsky & Associates law firm, wrote, "I would advise Liz not to send the memo at this time. A vigilant CEO would not have permitted this kind of discriminatory work environment to evolve in the first place. In short, the issues with which Liz is concerned would not exist at Vision unless Clark tacitly allowed them to develop. Clark cannot be trusted with Liz's message."[23] Jay M. Jackman, M.D., a private practice psychologist and business consultant, and Myra H. Strober, a labor economist at Stanford University, agreed that Liz should not send the memo: "As any good mountaineer will tell you, a successful ascent requires a good deal of preparation: choosing fellow climbers, ensuring team conditioning, assembling first-rate equipment, and hiring experienced guides. Raising issues of sexism with the CEO of a corporation requires similar preparation. Liz definitely should discuss the issues of gender stonewalling at Vision Software with Clark but not alone, not yet, and not by memo."[24]

Author and entrepreneur expert Joline Godfrey took a harder line. "After years of banging heads against glass ceilings, huge numbers of women are realizing that learning how to dress, getting the right degrees, and struggling to fit in are essentially fruitless exercises," she wrote. "Of a certain age and self-awareness, women who are weary of trying to adapt to environments in which they are not welcome are leaving to create companies that fit them. The woman who feels strongly enough to write a memo is in the process of breaking with an unfriendly culture. Whether she sends it or not is unimportant — the process of alienation has begun. And if she chooses not to spend another calorie of energy teaching lessons that companies have had over two decades to learn — and are in their own best interests — that's her prerogative."[25]

The case stirred controversy in businesses, colleges, and at conferences across the country. Women who thought Liz's memo a sincere, nonaggressive attempt to inform a CEO of a condition for women he might choose to change were shocked to learn that many people saw the memo quite differently. To many men, Liz was a "militant radical." Others saw her as "someone overreacting to minor events and causing trouble." They didn't get it. But they represent a significant number of men who believe women are "bitching" when they propose that their work is not taken seriously or that the company communication climate is hostile to women. A number of women were not altogether happy with Liz's memo either. They thought it too demure. "She ought to spell it out for him," a female marketing director proposed. "If you're going to fill him in, give him all the facts. Don't just list a few. And tell him what he ought to do about it too." Another female executive argued, "Liz is living in a dream world. You can't send memos to CEOs and expect them to say, 'Oh my, I didn't know this was happening. Let's put an end to it right now.' It just doesn't happen that way. If you're going to send a memo, send a tough one. Make sure he gets it. And be packed because you won't be there long."

This case stirred considerable debate because there are Lizes all over. They write memos and put them away in their desk drawers. Few speak up. There are unwritten rules against that, and there is always what many see as the awful possibility of being labeled a feminist. They acquiesce to an unwritten rule: Serious businesswomen do not involve themselves in gender issues. They stifle their own styles of communication even though most know that adopting male styles doesn't work. Whether Liz was sufficiently explicit or apparently naive in her hope that the CEO would respond positively to her memo, at least she took a chance. She reached the point many women reach where they can either speak up or leave. Several women like Liz whom I met when developing the case did both. They wrote memos and left shortly thereafter. Others stayed. Some of them will be introduced in future chapters. Among them are women who actually made a difference. Who risked the labels of feminist, radical, naive do-gooder to play a role in revising the communication climates of their companies.

MOVING TO THE NEXT STAGE

It is time to rewrite the communication rules or give up the game. In retrospect, women have learned that trying to be like men is exhausting and nonproductive. Demurring does not work either. As Kate Wilson, marketing director for the research division of a top office products company, explains: "We can all play by men's rules, but I'd like to think the next stage will allow women to be themselves. I've compromised along the way. I do less of it now. But you can't pull out all the stops at once."

For Kate and many women who have done well in a male work environment, communicating with men is becoming less and less a one-style endeavor. It involves blending what is comfortable with what is foreign. It involves, as Kate points out, deciding when to compromise and when not to: "There are times when you have to speak up. This requires being selective and knowing which people are not educable. Self-protection barriers are necessary. To avoid being personally hurt the barriers have to be there. But they come up and down." Sometimes you play it their way, sometimes you follow your own instincts and live with the results. Being fixated on one style is a recipe for discontent, if not failure. As Kate Wilson found, "Sometimes the path can't be smoothed, so you learn to ride the bumps. Other times, you take the floor, expect to be included, and let people know exactly what you want."

If the next stage is going to be defined in part by women, then it is time to stop thinking that working with people who speak a different language can be successful if you learn a few new phrases. Communication is complex. It is also a reciprocal activity. Each person's verbal or nonverbal action limits the choices of the other person or persons with whom she is interacting. If women are quiet when they should speak up, they send the wrong message. Their silence encourages others to repeat prior offensive behavior. The following story is a case in point.

A forty-two-year-old woman with only one year on the job stood up at a meeting to make what she considered an important point. When she sat down, a male senior colleague whispered to her, "Giving some mixed messages, aren't you?" Puzzled, she asked him to explain. "You're full of conviction," he said, "but you're showing a lot of leg in that skirt." She spent the next three weeks trying to decide how to respond. "If I tell him off," she thought, "I'll get on his wrong side. He'll take it personally and he'll think I overreacted." Ultimately she discovered that not nipping this kind of thing in the bud is a guarantee that it will happen again.

Her silence influenced his options. Had she spoken up, she might not have had to endure further insult. She did not, mostly for fear of offending a superior. But silence also communicates. In this case, it told him that she did not mind personal comments about her dress and body. In such situations, you have to decide what counts. And the answer is your credibility and integrity. He may be the nicest guy in the world but he's wrong. Whatever style you use, it's important to let him know that you're not about to knit booties while he undermines your work with lewd comments. Most women hesitate to take such steps, worrying that "he might get me later." Maybe he will. But think about it. He's getting you now. Later is later. If you manage the early problems, the later ones are often less virulent.

I've also discovered something that many women do not realize. In situations like the preceding one, men overhearing or observing often wonder why the woman hasn't spoken up. "I don't know why women take the insults" is a common observation among men. They know when one of their peers has stepped over the line. But they expect women to take some initiative to assure it doesn't happen again.

The 75 Percent Rule

I have a rule that works. It is based on over twenty years of studying communication, persuasion, and negotiation and a recognition that communication is truly a reciprocal activity. What people put into it influences what they get out of it. The rule is this: Each of us is at least 75 percent responsible for how people treat us. If you lie like a rug, people walk on you. If you run from a dog, it chases and bites. Taking a stand, even if you have to start small, is important because it sends the message Think before you speak to me!

Take the example of a female middle manager who returned from a business trip full of good news to share with her boss. After telling him about the successful meeting, she waited for him to join in her elation. Instead he said, "Fine. Just don't think this means you'll be gallivanting around the country every time there's a contract to negotiate." What would you say? She walked away angry. She should have spoken up then. Of course, hindsight is 20–20. But it's important to think on your feet. She could have challenged his use of the term "gallivanting" or point-blank asked him, "What are you talking about?" What most women forget is that there's simply no excuse for comments like this. Some men will tell you you're taking things too seriously or that you don't have a sense of humor. Most know better. The 75 percent rule applies here. You can let comments about your humor twist you in knots, as they do many women, or you can limit the offender's future options by doing something about it. Saying, "You might want to take a course in what's funny" is one option.

For women who prefer to avoid direct communication about offensive behavior, it's important to ask yourself whether the less direct approach has been doing you any good. If it has, stick with it. If not, then it's time for a change. It is important to recognize, however, that indirectness can be misinterpreted as a lack of conviction or indecisiveness.

A few years back one of my male colleagues did me a favor. He told me, "The reason why you get more of what you don't want than I do is because I tell them no." I responded, "I tell them no too." "It sounds that way to you," he said, "but not to men. You have to make it crystal clear. Start with a big fat NO. But don't say, 'No, I don't think so' or 'I'm not comfortable with that.' Just say flat out, 'NO, can't do it.' If you want to take a little edge off, tell them, 'Like to help but I just can't. Sorry.' Leave it at that. No explanation. When you explain, you leave them room to persuade you. So just make it absolutely clear and they'll back off. If you want to give in a little later on and be a hero, fine."

My male colleagues have been a constant source of information. They purposely or inadvertently introduced me to communication techniques they'd learned for survival. It didn't take long for me to realize that they speak a different language. The question is Should women talk like men in order to be understood? The answer is Sometimes yes, sometimes no. One of my colleagues from outside the Business School recently asked me where I learned to talk "the language." She'd observed at a meeting how I had translated the interests of women on campus into the lingo used by male administrators. They responded positively. Not because I had asked them for anything the other women hadn't mentioned, but because I had asked for it in their language.

I don't think women should do this all the time. Benjamin Franklin was right when he advised, "Everything in moderation." There is much to be said for nurturing variety in one's communication styles — taking an experimental approach to interactions with others. Laura Gschwandtner, editor-in-chief of *Personal Selling Power Magazine,* concurs: "I found out that when I spoke directly, like men with whom I work, people thought I was 'brassy' or 'a snob.' It didn't take long to learn that people form opinions about you that have nothing to do with who you are. Over time I've experimented with how I communicate. If I'm selling, I make a point of discovering how I'm received. Sometimes brash works. Sometimes it doesn't. I've taught myself to use a wide range rather than constraining myself to one style. It has worked well."

At the heart of most problems between men and women at work is the tendency to underestimate the complexity of communication, especially across genders. The situation is not improved when women adopt male styles and abdicate their own. It is miserable to be someone other than yourself all day. It is better to ask: "Am I making myself clear given who I'm dealing with." As the "showing a little leg in that skirt" story reveals, there are times when being direct is the best recourse. It's rarely necessary to deck someone to get your point across. But there are times when you have to pull out all the stops. If someone shows you up, insults or interrupts you more than once, you can let it keep happening or you can respond in a way that assures it won't happen again.

Communication is a complex activity. For women to make it to the top of traditional organizations, they are going to have to recognize that the two currently popular routes, keeping quiet while proving oneself and beating men at their own games, are not working. When it comes to the big-stakes game of senior management, women's communication strategies must be both sophisticated and variable — less focused on what men want, more focused on what works personally and professionally.

This book is intended to be a road map of worksite communication terrains leading to lofty levels. It is not about mimicking men, beating them at their games, or suppressing femininity. It is about methods for combating the quicksand of indifference that is causing women to exit traditional organizations in numbers this country cannot afford. It is about trading fear for knowledge and making it possible to work with men by communicating in ways rarely explored.

‖ 2 ‖

THE LANGUAGE OF EXCLUSION: CRACKING THE CODE

TO THE CASUAL OBSERVER, communication appears to be an uncomplicated endeavor easily mastered — especially when compared with finance and other quantitative disciplines that have monopolized the minds of businesses' managers and the schools that educate them. But to the trained eye, communication is like a chess game. Each player's moves limit or expand the options of the other. The skilled communicator is capable of selecting, from a repertoire of words and nonverbal behaviors, those that will influence the amateur to follow his lead. As with any game, considerable advantage accrues to those who are playing in familiar surroundings.

Women are no less adept than men at communication. But women are relative strangers to senior management and most have underestimated the threat their presence poses to the set of comfortable communication patterns men have developed — the "language" that ultimately separates leaders from nonleaders.

To the novice, this language may seem no more challenging than any other. The subtle changes that workplace language undergoes as its users move into senior positions often go unnoticed by those left behind. The "language" of leadership is one of exclusion in most companies. How effectively a woman manages meaning through language and adjusts to subtle changes as her status and that of her co-workers change plays a major role in determining how far and fast she may advance.

The best language teacher is experience and immersion in the culture of those who use it. The same holds true for work. In the early part of her career, a woman is not alone in her immersion in the culture of traditional male-dominated organizations. As she approaches senior positions, however, her venture becomes more and more a solo one. In the absence of other women and knowledgeable mentors, her induction is difficult. She is thrust into a challenging situation with much promise, but often little preparation for the interpersonal challenges that she will face. Subtle communication cues and underlying meanings, understood by most men with little conscious thought, are unfamiliar and discomforting codes for women.

In many cases, women are not privy to the thought processes that lie hidden behind the observable actions of men. "Men seem much more comfortable arguing with each other at a morning meeting and then playing golf together in the afternoon. They know how to put things behind them," an Executive MBA student in her early thirties explained to my class of sixty-two primarily male students. "That's not altogether true," replied a male classmate also in his thirties. "We may seem to put things behind us, but much of the time we're thinking, 'Just wait. Some day I'll get that SOB.' And most often that is exactly what happens."

The view that at work men push angry thoughts out of their minds when dealing with other men is a common one, although I've witnessed some nasty fights between men. In general, they prefer this approach to talking through details and exploring the intricacies of other people's choices. As Carol Gilligan wrote, their orientation is not as relational as that of women. Their focus is usually more on the task at hand. To women it looks as if they forgive each other after conflict, but in many cases nothing could be further from the truth. They've merely learned to direct their anger in ways that allow them to continue working with each other so work objectives can be achieved. Such reactions are second nature to them — far more mentally effortless than for women.

Harvard researcher Ellen Langer believes that people spend much of each day in a "mindless" state, avoiding excessive cognitive effort.[1]

Thinking and reasoning can be tiring. Thus, people think about their behaviors only when situations require them to do so. At other times, they slip into scripted behaviors that allow them to exert less cognitive effort than would be required if they had to really think about what to say or do each time a common situation arose. When men focus on tasks rather than relational issues, they do so according to scripts they've learned as children and adults. That other men have learned to cooperate in these scripts allows them to join in with little conscious effort.

Women haven't yet mastered many of these male scripts. They have relied largely on scripts that were developed back when relationships with men were purely social, not professional. Men have done the same. Now that women want to be treated as equals, not as cute little people who are good at "detail" work, these scripts have lost their utility. Nowhere in the common repertoire is there a comfortable set of scripts for male-female interactions when both are equal or when the woman is the boss.

Communication patterns between men and women have not kept pace with women's progress. Women are past ready for leadership positions, even in the largest companies, but the communication scripts they bring to work are often at odds with those that men are accustomed to using. With such an imperfect fit, the efforts of men and women to work together at senior levels have yielded disappointing results. Their communication is clumsy and often nonproductive. It leads to misunderstandings and, on the part of both women and men, alienation and anger.

IDENTIFYING DYSFUNCTIONAL COMMUNICATION PATTERNS (DCPS)

In the course of my research, working with companies to alter their communication climates, and sharing ideas with other women after conference presentations, I've repeatedly heard mentioned a set of dysfunctional communication patterns that is particularly problematic for women who want to get ahead in traditional organizations. Wherever I travel, even outside the United States, women describe these patterns as part of the quicksand of indifference and disregard that keeps them in low-paying and less prestigious positions than men. The following is an example.

A Common Dysfunctional Communication Pattern

Janet, a forty-year-old regional manager for a food products company, has learned of an informal meeting that took place without her. She was the only product-launch committee member absent. Three male peers made some important decisions without her. Janet believes that she should have been present at the meeting or at least been told of her peers' ideas before they became formal decisions. There is no animosity between Fred and Janet, so she cannot understand why he, as committee chair, would allow a meeting to take place in her absence.

> *Janet:* I felt left out of the planning of this project, Fred. The meeting was held without my knowledge.
> *Fred:* Now, Janet, let's not make this a personal thing. Frank, Bill, and I happened to run into each other, so we got some work done.
> *Janet:* But I am on the planning team. You could have run it by me.
> *Fred:* You shouldn't waste your energy on this, Janet. It's nothing. Don't feel bad.
> *Janet:* It's happened several times.
> *Fred:* Getting a little paranoid, aren't we?
> *Janet:* I just want to be kept informed.
> *Fred:* Okay, Janet. Okay. It's no big deal.

Janet is trying to make sure her input on a project is not overlooked. Being left out of important decisions is something women experience often at work. When they complain, they are often told they are making too much of a small oversight.

Women who have been in such conversations report that nothing they say changes the outcome. "They just leave me out of the next meeting" is a common complaint. "Then I have to confront them on it, which makes me look like a whiner." Part of the reason for the repetitive nature of these destructive interactions is that the women involved have not learned communication strategies for turning them around. Janet may sound like a whiner because she is depending on Fred to provide a reasonable excuse. Since he doesn't have one that will satisfy her, he belittles her concern.

The interaction between Janet and Fred is an example of one type of dysfunctional communication pattern — exclusionary. Janet had been excluded from participation in an important informal meeting, and the conversation that followed merely increased her exclusion. Janet unwittingly contributed to the pattern by letting Fred control the direction and substance of the interaction. She based her comments to Fred on rules of equality and fair play. But Fred enacted a script that diminished her claims as irrelevant and overstated — failing that, he would have had to address them. He thus had a vested interest in convincing her that she had misinterpreted the situation.

This is not to suggest that men have consciously searched for ways to make women feel irrelevant. Fred's actions follow from two common stereotypes of women — they have a tendency to take things personally, and they talk about relational issues rather than task expectations. Janet confirmed these stereotypes by saying that she felt "left out." She did not voice her outrage or point out that Fred, Bill, and Frank had behaved in an unprofessional, devious, self-serving fashion. Had she taken that approach, and made it clear to Fred, he likely would not have responded to her in the way he did. Her opening line, "I felt left out . . . ," set the conversation on a personal path, focused attention on her emotions, and gave Fred the opening he needed to talk to her about how she was responding emotionally rather than what he did wrong. Janet's next response personalized the issue again: "But I am on the planning team. You could have run it by me." This statement is more a request than an assertion. Fred was asked to do something about the past that he cannot do. Janet did not address the real problem: Fred, Bill, and Frank's assumption that it is acceptable to conduct business when a team member is absent and uninformed.

Since Janet focused this conversation on her own emotional state rather than the infraction of her colleagues, Fred was free to mention her feelings by saying, "Don't feel bad." He then engaged in amateur psychoanalysis, "Getting a little paranoid, aren't we?" Janet's choice of words influenced Fred's communication options. He focused on Janet's reaction rather than on the issue of meeting without the knowledge of the absent committee member.

As the exchange between Janet and Fred indicates, men like Fred don't get it yet, but neither do women like Janet. She became enmeshed in a dysfunctional communication pattern because the real issues were never addressed. There is nothing inherently wrong with mentioning feelings when seeking to rectify an upsetting series of events. But in this case, Janet was talking with Fred — a card-carrying member of the unenlightened. In such cases, it is important to have a variety of communication strategies available. To the extent that a woman does not have communication options, the likelihood is high of her slipping into a pattern that leads nowhere or threatens her career.

How Janet should have responded depends in part on her style, which we'll discuss at length later on. But Janet could have benefited by asking herself two questions before speaking with Fred: (1) What is the problem? (2) What do I want? Had Janet identified the problem as the inappropriateness of Fred's actions, she would have avoided starting the conversation by describing her own feelings. Instead of saying, "I felt left out of the planning of this project, Fred. The meeting was held without my knowledge," she might have said, "Fred, no more meetings without me." Simple and to the point. Not personal, not emotional. If her answer to question 2 is that she wants to be included in future meetings, then this simple statement takes care of that as well. If Fred followed her opening comment with an attempt to direct the conversation toward a defense of his position or a discussion of what he sees as her paranoia, her response should be: "None of that is relevant, Fred. No personal attacks intended or necessary. I'm on the team, I should be at the meetings. It's simple."

TAKING BACK CONTROL

Judy B. Rosener's 1990 research published in the *Harvard Business Review* identifies male-female communication style differences. She found that women "encourage participation, share power and information, enhance other people's self worth, and get others excited about their work."[2] Men do these things too, but women tend to do them more often. This and other studies indicate that women and men differ in their preferred styles of communicating leadership and power.

Women talk about relational issues more than men. Like Janet in the above scenario, they often appeal to fair play and refrain from aggressive personal attacks. They engage in what Erving Goffman describes as "tact" — hinting at the real issues to avoid negative interpersonal consequences. The hinter sends a message that is deniable. Janet hinted that Fred, Bill, and Frank had acted in an unacceptable, inappropriate manner, but she did not state this. She avoided the impression of confrontation. According to Goffman, each person influences the course of conversation by eliciting impressions — performing behaviors that lead others to think of him in a certain way:

> He may wish them to think highly of him, or think that he thinks highly of them, or to perceive how in fact he feels toward them or to obtain no clear-cut impression; he may wish to insure sufficient harmony so that the interaction can be sustained, or to defraud, get rid of, confuse, mislead, antagonize, or insult them.[3]

Janet's desire to preserve harmony or perhaps her predisposition to do so was stronger than her desire to create a clear-cut impression. As a result, Fred took the conversation in a direction not useful to Janet's goal of preventing such exclusionary practices in the future.

There is considerable value to the harmonious communication styles preferred by most women. But it is one thing to prefer certain communication styles and quite another to be stuck with them. For women who haven't expanded their communication repertoires, the advantage of knowing a few styles well is outweighed by the complexity of the task before them. Interaction techniques can be the means by which leadership is achieved or they can result in the communicator being ignored, excluded, and kept back.

The Value of Speaking Up

Everyone learns how to communicate in commonly experienced situations. When new situations are encountered, many people develop communication skills and styles to meet the new demands. These people are more likely to succeed than those who cling to old ways. For women, the most limiting of the old ways is a tendency to equate speaking up with conflict and adjectives such as unfeminine, undesirable, disruptive, and career-limiting.

Anne Huff, a business professor at the University of Colorado, believes that women often act like "wives of the organization." They see their role as supportive and noncomplaining. They fail to speak up or to leave situations, even when these are the most appropriate actions.[4]

Dysfunctional communication patterns can't be eradicated unless women are willing to risk altering them. When an interaction emanates from an outmoded stereotype, speaking up and exiting are two approaches women can take to improve the communication cultures in which they work. Unfortunately, many women think speaking up requires physically leaving their jobs, as indicated by many of the responses to Liz's memo in Chapter 1. But speaking up need not be abrasive and exiting need not be physical.

Speaking up has gotten an undeserved bad reputation, especially for women. The truth is that a wide range of communication strategies exists between demure and abrasive. Clinging to either end of the range is a recipe for failure.

Many women worry that assertive behavior will upset men and lead to disfavor. What they have failed to consider is that they aren't exactly in favor anyway. Letting others label your behaviors, direct the course of your interactions, and exclude, interrupt, and devalue you is not better than upsetting a few men now and then.

Consider the freedom boorish men have to be themselves in leadership positions. They have not been kept from senior management. In fact, *Fortune* magazine celebrates their existence with a special edition devoted in 1993 to "America's Toughest Bosses." An excerpt from this edition refers to John Connors, CEO of Hill Holiday:

> So extreme are Connors's outbursts that they have become known around the office as Jack Attacks. During one, Connors called in a young employee who hadn't collected a bill from a client. He started screaming so loudly that the kid was left literally shaking. Says a former employee, who witnessed that Jack Attack: "With Jack there was one standard and recurring theme: 'I do everything, and no one else does anything around here.' Adds an executive who used to work for Connors, "If you look up the word 'control freak' in the dictionary, there ought to be a picture of Jack right next to it."[5]

Then there is what *Fortune* writer Brian Dumaine identified as the "Inquisitor" type of CEO, who is "aggressive and exacting when seeking information, often to a fear-inducing fault." The man who epitomizes this type is T. J. Rodgers, chief executive officer of Cypress Semiconductor. According to Dumaine:

> Refreshingly honest about his punishing management style, Rodgers says that working at Cypress is like "crawling through a muddy battlefield." Once, when employees complained about long hours, Rodgers dug out old Army cots and pillows that he and the other company founders used in the early 1980s when some literally slept in the office. Rodgers then set up the cots outside the bathrooms to remind people how easy they have it, working only 12- to 14-hour days."[6]

According to Abraham Zaleznik, professor emeritus of leadership at Harvard Business School: "Tough is passé. Today you're dealing with a variety of head games. That's where the cruelty is." Tough of the Connors and Rodgers type is passé. But a lot of people haven't gotten that message yet.

The message of the *Fortune* article is that men aren't expected to weigh the implications of their every move. While the article also describes a tough female boss, Linda Wachner, CEO of Warnaco, the implication is that macho tactics are okay for men doing the right things. In a climate honoring "control freaks" and "psycho bosses from hell," it is easy to see how low-key approaches, preferred more by women than men, could be misinterpreted as indicative of less than leadership potential.

Warren Bennis, professor, author, and management consultant, asked by *Psychology Today* for his recommendation to people working for tough, insensitive bosses who don't encourage employee growth and development, replied: "I think you should talk to the boss directly, one-on-one. And if that doesn't work, go around and talk to other people and maybe even to the boss' boss." Bennis acknowledges that people may have to be ready to leave, but he argues that for leaders, managers, middle-men and -women, "The best people also have a bias toward action; they keep saying, 'You're never going to get anywhere if you keep sitting in the dugout.' The only way you're going to succeed, ultimately, in whatever you do, is to get up there and take your swings. And sometimes that means taking a swing at someone else, someone who you think is doing something wrong or dangerous for the company."[7]

Speaking up need not lead to conflict, especially if the method used avoids personal attack. If it does lead to conflict, that could be good. Conflict is normal. Consistent harmony in human relations is a sure sign of mediocrity. It's important to shake things up now and then.

Bennis describes the quiet, nonconfrontational approach to bad work situations as follows: "It's not unlike staying in a bad marriage because you're frightened by the prospect of being too old to remarry and not being in a financial position to strike out on your own again. So you stuff it all down and say I'm going to just stay in a lousy relationship because the alternatives are worse."

When women wait for their bosses to treat them with respect, they waste precious time. Worrying that he'll get angry is one-sided. It diminishes the importance of the anger the woman feels and places the blame on her when it may well belong to him. Some women have taken the opposite course to an extreme. This is not effective. I've met women who have chosen to prove themselves by adopting characteristically male styles. This is just as limiting as being stuck with only demure styles. Consider, for example, the style of Hewlett-Packard engineer Sara Westendorf.

> Of course, when you're a female working in a nearly all-male environment, you have to expect resistance. There is always going to be a certain amount of sexism. But I try to turn the situation around by using humor — and dishing the sexism right back. If we're in a meeting and one of the men who is arguing with me begins to get hot under the collar, I'll say, "You know, John, you're getting awfully emotional. I guess it must be that time of the month for you." The people in the room usually break out in laughter. The person I direct it to may not be amused, but he'll have to chuckle along with it.[8]

There is no doubt that being a female engineer with mostly male co-workers is no walk in the park. Westendorf had to develop survival skills. But exclusive adoption of styles at the abrasive end of the demure-to-abrasive range of communication strategies can be just as limiting as those at the opposite end. Consider Westendorf's second example of turning the situation around.

I used a similar technique once with a former boss, who was known for being a womanizer. When I submitted recommendations for raises for some of the employees I managed, he was dismayed because I had not given an increase to one of his favorite female software engineers. "Oh," he said, "she's got such great legs, and a cute smile. We need to keep her around. Let's give her a raise." Then he moved on down the list of names and said he wasn't sure that he approved of the raise I was putting in for a male engineer. Without missing a beat, I said, "That engineer is so well-hung you wouldn't believe it. I can't afford to lose guys like that in my department. That raise has got to stay in." My boss chuckled. I think he suddenly realized he was suggesting giving a woman a raise for something that had nothing to do with her work. He let me have the raise (but he gave one to the woman, too).

Stories like this attract press attention. Controversial women, the ones who don't fit the mold, are press-worthy. But in the everyday world of work, abrasive communication is no more effective on a regular basis than demure communication.

Getting Past Fear

There are many women who are quite skilled at communication but hesitate to apply what they know. For women with an extensive repertoire of communication strategies who refuse to perfect and utilize them, most often the problem is fear. Few things are so constraining as fear; it shackles self-confidence and compromises self-esteem. Both men and women experience considerable fear in organizations across the United States, but women are especially fearful. The reason is occasionally economic but more often, especially among senior women, fear exists because they've abdicated control of their symbolic environments. Neither are they full partners in the business communication around them nor do they repel derogatory labels and redirect hurtful interactions with men. They are still worried that they might be seen as "missing the mark," "not a team player," "needing more experience," "still transitioning," and/or "too sensitive." Their fear has been like an albatross about their necks. Like the Ancient Mariner, they won't be free to excel until they take back some control. This means, in many cases, speaking up in ways that revise the communication climate that has held them back or exiting interactions destined to be destructive.

TURNING AROUND DYSFUNCTIONAL COMMUNICATION PATTERNS

Management expert Michael Porter poses two questions to those planning organizational change: Is this industry profitable? How can I change it to make it more so? He recommends that people employ their core competencies and effective actions to bring about change.[9] For many women, work has not been as profitable as they expected. Their core competency is a predisposition to communicate in ways that improve and maintain relationships. But they need to learn a variety of effective communication actions for redirecting or terminating dysfunctional communication patterns. The following scenario demonstrates what to look for and how to change a negative interaction.

> *Michael:* You came on a bit strong in that meeting.
> *Jessica:* I was just trying to make a point.
> *Michael:* Well, you sure did that.
> *Jessica:* Do you think I overdid it?
> *Michael:* It isn't what I think that counts.
> *Jessica:* Did Al say anything to you about what I said?
> *Michael:* He didn't have to. Didn't you see his eyes?

This conversation depends on two things for its existence: Michael's and Jessica's willingness to participate. The thirty-two-year-old woman who provided this DCP was fearful that her assertive behavior would be used as a reason to label her a troublemaker. She is an aerospace manager surrounded by men. She shared her frustration with me: "If I'm quiet, they ignore me. If I speak up, they drop by to tell me how unwelcome or surprising my comments were. I'm worried they'll decide that I'm too much trouble to keep around."

Obviously she cares what her peers and superiors think. Why shouldn't she? Her job is at stake. What she hasn't learned, however, is that the more worried she becomes about the perceptions of others, the more vulnerable she is to their criticisms. People categorize and label other people's actions. According to attribution theorist Fritz Heider, people seek sufficient reasons or explanations for the behaviors of others. They do this "to make possible a more or less stable, predictable, and controllable world."[10]

Categorizing actions, especially surprising ones, is part of being human. When then presidential candidate Bill Clinton appeared to change his mind on some issues during the campaign, he was described as a "waffler." When Congresswoman Patricia Schroeder shed tears while announcing her decision not to run for president, she was criticized for acting like "an emotional woman." When Jessica spoke up at a meeting, Michael, and perhaps other men as well, decided she had (for a woman) come on too strong. If stereotypes are conveniently located in memory, they are called upon to help with the categorization process. What people often forget is that each of us can choose to accept the categories and labels, to agonize over them, or to reject them. Words are imprisoning if the recipient of criticism imbues them with the power to make her miserable.

In the DCP above, Jessica gave that power to Michael. When she said, "I was just trying to make a point," her defensive stance signaled to Michael that she was willing to participate in the DCP he had started. When she later said, "Do you think I overdid it?" she confirmed his control over the definition of her actions and reinforced the direction of the DCP. She prolonged the process by asking, "Did Al say anything about it?"

This interaction would have been quite different had Jessica been unwilling to let Michael's definition of her actions survive unscathed. Consider this possibility:

Michael: You came on a bit strong in that meeting.
Jessica: Somebody had to. The project is too important to worry about making everyone feel cozy.

In hindsight, this may seem a simple solution, but simple makes the point. And as one female lawyer who describes herself as having "been around and seen it all" told me, the problem for most women is thinking of a good, simple response on the spot. "I can think of things I should have said on the way home, but I need to learn how to stop offenders in their tracks with as few words as possible. Waiting a few days doesn't work."

In the above example, Jessica's response is swift, short, and unexpected. It pulls the two communicators out of the scripted DCP and into new territory — one more positive and professional. It also conveys that Jessica is confident and that she has a persuasive, legitimate, work-related reason for her actions. Her conviction signals to Michael that she won't yield to his definition of her actions at the meeting.

People often retry initiating a DCP when others have refused to cooperate. Despite Jessica's assertive reply, Michael might try to throw her off track with this statement:

Michael: Well, you sure made your point.

Again, Jessica has a choice. She can participate in a negative DCP or respond in a way that is unexpected, positive, and likely to bring the interaction to a close. The following is an example:

Michael: Well, you sure made your point.
Jessica: Thank you.

Jessica has refused to participate in the DCP. The likelihood of Michael trying again is not high at this point. Jessica is opting out of the dysfunctional pattern, refusing to let old scripts dictate her present behavior. Even if Jessica is concerned about the reactions others at the meeting might have had to her assertive comments, she needn't convey the message that she is worried. It just encourages people to continue emphasizing differences in a negative manner.

It's possible that Michael will consider her "Thank you" response abrupt. She might smile as she says it, to soften the blow. But this is risky. Too much or too sweet a smile could negate the impact of her attempt to reject his definition. He may pay more attention to the smile than to the message she really wants him to get. Whatever approach Jessica adopts, the important thing is refusing to allow Michael sole discretion in labeling her actions.

DETERMINING THE CONTROL DIRECTION

Research by communication scholars Frank Millar and Edna Rogers demonstrates how communication patterns can lead to erroneous perceptions. Millar and Rogers assess the directionality of communicators' inputs.[11] For example, if a comment is made in an assertive manner as if to define and control the situation, it is labeled a "one-up" move, designated by an arrow pointing upward (↑). Comments that indicate acceptance of the other person's definition or control are "one-down" moves, labeled with arrows pointed downward (↓). In the interchange between Michael and Jessica, all of Michael's comments are one-up moves. All of Jessica's are one-down moves as seen below:

> *Michael:* You came on a bit strong in that meeting. (↑)
> *Jessica:* I was just trying to make a point. (↓)
> *Michael:* Well, you sure did that. (↑)
> *Jessica:* Do you think I overdid it? (↓)
> *Michael:* It isn't what I think that counts. (↑)
> *Jessica:* Did Al say anything to you about what I said? (↓)
> *Michael:* He didn't have to. Didn't you see his eyes? (↑)

Michael's last comment is a question, but it is a one-up question — more a rhetorical question than one seeking a reply. It is clear that Jessica has placed herself in the one-down position in this entire interaction. The control belongs to Michael, and so he acquires the right to define her actions. Her input is consistently subservient to his. The exchange is a complementary one where one person is dominant, the other yielding.

Millar and Rogers's method of analysis is quite useful. It clearly demonstrates how the direction of Jessica's replies to Michael allow a pattern to continue and an impression to come out of it that does not facilitate her progress as a professional. By contrast, were she unwilling to accept his definition of her actions, Jessica could have provided her own. The following is an example:

> *Michael:* You sure came on a bit strong in that meeting. (↑)

Jessica: Somebody had to. The project is too important to worry about making everyone feel cozy. (↑)

In this scenario, Jessica matches Michael's one-up move with a one-up move of her own. She negates his label, redirects the interaction, and redefines what occurred in a manner that focuses on the task rather than on her. With one verbal expression she recoups the right to define her own actions.

Some ways in which women are treated differently do not involve verbal expression. Marilyn, a bank executive, told me of an appalling experience. She had arrived late to a dinner at a club that had only recently (and begrudgingly) accepted women. As she approached the table, a young man at the far end jumped up, ran around the large, oblong table, grabbed her chair, and pulled it out just as she was about to be seated. "I couldn't believe it, " she said. "He nearly killed himself getting to my chair. I was embarrassed for me and for him." She explained that he was new to the club and had probably wanted to make a good impression. To avoid future displays of athletic chivalry, she did approach him after the dinner to let him know that it would not be necessary on future occasions for him to rush around the table to pull out her chair. "I was gentle about it," she explained. "I know he was trying to do the right thing. But I wasn't about to have men leaping over tables upon my arrival."

Had she not informed the young man that his actions were unnecessary, the situation would have continued to occur. In this case, Marilyn took responsibility for her part of the potential repeat of this DCP. She intercepted it before it became commonplace.

For those women or those times when a one-up response to a one-up move seems too abrupt, there is also the choice of a "one-across" move. This involves saying or doing something that is neither one-up nor one-down, but neutral. For example, to Michael's statement "You came on a bit strong in that meeting," Jessica might answer, "It's interesting that you interpreted it that way." In this case, Jessica has not abruptly one-uped Michael nor has she contributed to the downward spiral by a one-down move. She has merely mentioned that his response is interesting. She has opted out from taking a stand or yielding. Such statements are one-across moves, designated by an arrow pointed to the side (→). They are leveling moves intended neither to accept nor confront the other party's attempt to define the situation.

Using both one-up and one-across moves changes the nature of the entire interaction:

Michael: You came on a bit strong in that meeting. (↑)
Jessica: It's interesting that you interpreted it that way. (→)
Michael: Well, you certainly made your point. (↑)
Jessica: The project is an important one. It's no time to mince words. (↑)
Michael: I suppose you're right. (↓)

The lesson here is that people have the power to define the actions of others to the extent they are allowed to do so. Labels are powerful things. And whether women work at junior or senior levels, they tend to fear them. But it's fear that allows dysfunctional patterns of communication to continue. Once women recognize that they can redirect interactions harmful to their careers, they become empowered to manage the perceptions of others and their own self-perceptions as well.

‖ 3 ‖

GETTING AT THE SUBTLE STUFF

REGINALD STRONGBROW ARRIVED at his office at 8:02 A.M. The traffic had been heavy. As he sat down at his desk, his boss, Bill Simmons, V.P. of operations, stopped in the doorway. "Strongbrow, you're looking tired today," he said, more as an observation than an expression of concern. "Family problems?" Reginald was taken aback. He didn't feel tired, and there were no family problems. Bill awaited a reply. "No. I'm fine," Reginald said. "Okay," Bill replied as he started to move on. "Get some rest." Reginald sat at his desk wondering whether he looked tired and what Bill's comment about his family had meant.

Reginald glanced up at the clock. It was now 8:30. Attempting to put the remark behind him, Reginald began to peruse the mail on his desk. He came across a copy of the division's newsletter. The front page carried a photo and story about his project team. Reginald was not included in the photo, nor was he mentioned in the story. Newsletter in hand, he walked down the hall to the office of John Smith, project coordinator. "If you have a moment," Reginald said, "I just saw the story in the newsletter." Smith looked at the newsletter in Reginald's hand and quickly replied, "Oh, that spur-of-the-moment thing. The editor wanted a photo of the team, so we got together and let them take one. I think you were away that morning. We had to meet a print deadline. No big deal though. Right?" This wasn't the first time Reginald had been overlooked, but he decided not to belabor the issue. "No big deal," he said. "Yeah," Smith added, "it isn't even a good photo, and the story is worse. You're lucky you got out of it."

As Reginald returned to his office, he met the division secretary, who said, "You have a meeting with Frank Pillar in ten minutes." Pillar, the CEO, wanted an update on the project team's progress. Reginald entered the conference room early so he could prepare his thoughts. Pillar entered with Bill Simmons at his side. "Hey there, Reginald," Pillar said, smiling. "Bill, check out Reginald's new suit . . . and what a tie! We must be paying him too much." Simmons laughed aloud. Reginald smiled. He could take a joke. Yet he wondered what Pillar had meant. They certainly weren't paying him what he deserved. He considered himself to have good taste and he never bought anything too stylish. Reginald decided to let the comment pass, thinking, "It was probably harmless — no real meaning or message."

During the meeting, Reginald offered his opinion on a project item with which he was intimately familiar. He no sooner began his comment than Bill interrupted him. "Let me just finish this point," Reginald said. The interrupter yielded and Reginald began again to explain his position. Again Bill interrupted him with "I want to be sure we get some closure on this today." Reginald didn't hear much of Bill's remarks beyond that point. He was busy dealing with his annoyance and frustration.

The rest of the day was uneventful. Reginald finished some work between thoughts about what Bill had meant by his early morning comments, about having been excluded from the team photo and story, and then being interrupted. At 6 P.M. he prepared to leave for the day. Bill appeared in the doorway. "Before you go, I want to mention you don't have to worry about the Japan trip. Mike will be going." Reginald's mouth fell open. He had planned on making the trip to Japan, an important one for the company. "What do you mean?" was the only response Reginald could think of at the moment. "Well, with your two kids and Mary working, we didn't think you'd want to be away for a week. Don't give it another thought. It's a done deal. See you tomorrow."

As Reginald walked to his car, he felt drained. "This can't go on," he told himself. "Another day like this and I'm out of here."

Reginald Strongbrow had just experienced what is, for many women, a typical day at work. There is, of course, no Reginald Strongbrow, but if men were to experience the subtle put-downs and frequent quips that keep women feeling unwelcome and devalued, they too would be leaving organizations in large numbers.

As Brenda Snyder, the twenty-eight-year-old outspoken president of US West Women, a lobby for the company's 36,148 women, explained in 1992, "On a surface level for the majority of the corporations, not discriminating against women is rewarded. You just don't hear certain kinds of things. We have come far. But the next mountain is harder to climb, and that is all the stuff you can't see, can't feel, can't touch, but it's there. It's the subtle, subliminal discrimination."[1]

The stuff women can't see, feel, or touch are interactions that leave them feeling ignored, excluded, patronized, insulted, or undermined. Bringing what now seems subliminal out into the open for evaluation and revision is what this chapter is about. DCPs are at the heart of the "stuff" working women can't see, feel, or touch. Identifying and altering them is the only way women will reach leadership positions in significant numbers.

To do so, women must take control over what is said to them and how they're treated. It's time women countered some one-up moves with one-up moves of their own. No more waiting for younger men to be different from their fathers. No more smiling at offense. It is time to confront the obvious: Women will not be welcomed into senior-level positions until and unless they start acting like they belong there. No one expects U.S. Olympians Bonnie Blair or Nancy Kerrigan to walk onto the ice thinking they don't belong there and hoping they won't offend the people who do. That is not a winning posture. Yet it's one many women still cling to — the "grateful to be here" approach.

It bears repeating that women are not only valuable to business, they are indispensable. They have reached critical mass. What remains is for them to believe it and to develop the communication skills for success. It's time to stop wondering about disparaging remarks and to start responding on the spot. It's time to cease worrying about being thought humorless for rejecting offensive jokes. And it's time to expect to be included in important events and selected for key assignments, whether or not you've decided to be a mother.

DISMISSIVE DCPS

The most common dysfunctional pattern of male-female interaction at work involves dismissing women by interrupting, talking over, or ignoring them. "It's as if I'm not there much of the time," a female marketing manager explained to me during a presentation I was making on women reaching the top of their organizations. "I'll say something. They'll look at me and move on as if I hadn't said anything. It's unbelievable." Another woman in the same company described a similar pattern: "I start to say something and they just interrupt. They might say, 'I get the picture, so . . .' and go on with their thoughts or just dismiss what I'm in the process of saying with 'That's not going to work.' How does he know? If he'd let me finish he might learn something. It infuriates me."

Research indicates that men interrupt women more than women interrupt men.[2] It's habit. Women often contribute to the pattern by not insisting upon regaining the floor. They also speak more softly and sometimes take longer to get to the point, so men get impatient. Men are accorded greater credibility as a rule, so people are willing to hear them out. These factors culminate to create environments where women are not heard. They are invisible at some meetings. Tired of being talked over and dismissed, many resort to silence.

Silent retreat perpetuates the problem. It's important to speak up. "I'd like to finish my thoughts" is one possibility. "You may not have meant to interrupt me, Al, but you did" is another. Some women regain the floor by saying, "Let's get back to what I was describing earlier" or "This is important, so I'm not letting it drop."

Nonverbal displays of dominance and status are important here. Men are used to violating the personal space of women. Research shows that women have smaller zones of personal space than men, are touched more often than they touch, sit in "ladylike" ways. Men have a wider range of possible stances indicative of higher status and greater comfort. Women are also more tolerant of personal space violations. They are usually smaller than men, speak in higher pitches, show greater receptivity through eye contact often associated with lower status, and they smile more often.[3]

There are times when these "feminine" ways of communicating are effective. Velma Moore, a real estate agent, told me, "I find that my supportive, understanding approach pays off with my bosses. The two of them are often at each other's throats. They argue all the time. I listen to them and then say, 'Now wait a minute. The two of you aren't disagreeing as much as you think.' I help them reach an understanding. They appreciate it."

I asked Moore, "Do you think this will get you promoted?" She paused and then said, "You know, I don't know. Maybe it won't." As we later discussed, it's important for women to realize that while the short term rewards for "feminine" ways of communicating are often appealing, the real question is whether relying exclusively on them might lead to misinterpretations of your ability to handle difficult situations, including conflict.

The ways we communicate convey meaning. To the extent that a boss sees a woman subordinate's actions as indicative of nurturance and kindness but not of assertiveness and leadership capability, he is likely to treat her ideas as not deserving of attention and fail to seriously consider her for promotion as well. If his misinterpretation of her communication style is not brought to his attention, she is denied access to senior levels.

Xerox Corporation found that women were being talked over in what several of their employees described to me as a command-and-control environment. It's a top-down, hierarchical, respect-upward-but-not-across-and-downward type of work environment. Xerox senior management decided to give all their people the right to be heard. As one female manager explained, "I can now tell a senior manager who interrupts me, 'You just shut me out.' He'll stop talking and let me finish. He knows that's expected of him now. So, no matter who he is, he has to respect my right to express my opinion."

At Xerox, this practice brought a common pattern of interaction to the forefront of people's minds. Northrop Corporation instituted a similar procedure. At meetings managers who interrupted had to put a few dollars into a charity fund. Shirley Peterson, Northrop Grumman vice president for ethics and business conduct, believes that the process really helped: "People didn't realize they were interrupting each other. They'd just get carried away with their own ideas. We had times when someone would throw his money onto the table and say, 'I can't take it, I have to interrupt.' It put some humor into the learning process."

Corporate rules for altering DCPs may prove useful. But in time, as happened at Northrop, the charm wears off and people return to their old ways. In such cases, the responsibility rests on the shoulders of individuals. Women and men must make concerted efforts to disallow Dismissive DCPs. The best way is to develop a repertoire of phrases that allow people to regain the floor. For example, "I'd like to hear Frances finish her thought" or "You're like a bull in a china shop, Jack. Let Madeline complete her sentence" can be used to assist others. For the person whose allies are absent or quiet, the following floor-regaining phrases are useful: "You guys can hear me out now or never hear the end of it. Your choice," "Sit back, Bill, I plan to finish my thought this time," or "Take a breath, Larry, I'd like to get a word in edgewise."

Style preferences, status of the offender, degree of offense, intentionality, and fear of retaliation enter into women's response choices. Most women prefer to avoid alienating co-workers with direct comebacks to interruptions and dismissals. Some are even willing to wait for the retirement or death of the offenders to bring an end to sexism. Life is much too short for that. Besides, there is a wide range of responses to offensive behaviors. Among them, demure silence is the least effective.

Passed Over

Women are also dismissed when they are overlooked for promotion. "It happened to me," said Marion Spicer, a thirty-two-year-old manager at a small executive search company. "One time they promoted a guy to manager of the division I'd been holding together. He lacked experience. Every time he made a decision, he had to come to me first. I was the invisible manager making all the decisions but getting none of the pay. It was crazy. In time they figured it out. By then we had more women and they had to promote some of us. But many good people left in the process, and the rest of us still remember and wonder if those days won't return."

Notice the phrase "In time they figured it out." Why wait for that? When I ask that question, many women say, "It just doesn't sound right to whine about a situation like that" or "You don't want to be labeled a complainer." There is truth to the common belief that people don't like chronic complainers and whiners. But it isn't necessary to whine. And a legitimate complaint worded in a nonpersonal manner is better than silence. Marion could have refused to help the fledgling manager look good. I haven't met many men who provide constant assistance to former peers promoted to positions they wanted. Yet many women do this. What the company gets is a two-for-one deal. They get the woman's expertise and a satisfied male.

Spicer was concerned that she would appear a "spoilsport" if she did not help. And she might have had she refused to help at all. But she didn't have to prop him up on a day-to-day basis.

Losing Credit

Another means of dismissing women involves stealing their ideas. To women it seems amazing, but Clara Ferris, training director for a high-tech firm, thinks men often don't see it as stealing: "Women are very careful to include other people in their proposals. They'll say, 'As Mark mentioned earlier' or 'Chuck's idea is key here.' They give credit. Sometimes to a fault. Men don't go to great lengths to make sure people are credited, so it looks like they're stealing an idea when they don't mention the original source."

Here's an alternative explanation: They're so used to not listening to women that they probably half hear an idea when a woman presents it. They think it came from their own brain. In other cases they know she won't speak up to retrieve ownership, so they usurp her thoughts and call them their own. Whatever the reason, it is infuriating.

Whether ideas are stolen from women purposely or inadvertently is less important than how women respond when it happens. When I ask women, "What did you do about it?" most reply, "At the time I just fumed" or "You can't blurt out, 'That was my idea.' It sounds like you're grabbing individual attention." These are dysfunctional responses. They merely perpetuate a bad situation.

Here are a few functional responses.

"Hey, Tom. That was my idea. Hands off. You're ruining it."
"Tom, get your own idea, that one was mine. When I proposed that
plan I had something slightly different in mind."
"I'm taking that idea back. You guys are butchering it."
"That plan sounds a lot like the one I mentioned earlier."

There are times when retrieving stolen ideas is not worth the effort.
But when big stakes are involved, it is unwise to let ideas pass quietly
into the hands of others. For those who abhor what some women have
described to me as "making a scene," there is always the behind-closed-
doors approach. A visit to the office of the person who stole the idea
might work just as well as exposing his folly in public. The following
repertoire of approaches ranges from direct to subtle.

DIRECT: I have just five words to say about your usurping my idea in
   there today: Don't let it happen again!
STRONG: We can work well together, Jim. Just remember to give credit
   where it's due. By the end of the meeting, I think everyone thought
   my project upgrade idea was yours. You know, two can play that
   game.
MODERATE: I don't know what you were thinking in that meeting today, Jim. I'd appreciate at least a footnote next time you borrow one
   of my ideas.
MILD: Jim, you might have directed some credit my way in that
   meeting.

Idea stealing and credit grabbing are on the increase. It's important
to learn how to handle such situations. According to the *Wall Street
Journal,* competition for jobs is fostering conditions conducive to back
stabbing.[4] Idea and credit snatching is a form of back stabbing when
it is purposeful. You have to locate the source and end it quickly. The
price of doing anything less can be high.

RETALIATORY DCPS

During a task force meeting I'd been invited to attend as a consultant,
the mostly female group of managers from across the country focused
their discussion on the slow pace of female promotions in this stereo

products company. A male manager in his mid-thirties who had been conspicuously silent for hours finally spoke up. Apparently tired of watching his female colleagues struggle to identify reasons why women had not reached the top of this mid-sized international company, he said, "Let me tell you what's really bothering a lot of us. Most of the men I know got burned one time or another by a woman. They haven't forgotten that. Women may have dumped them in elementary school or in college. Whenever it happened, it hurt. I remember when a girl came up to me in the fifth grade and said, 'Kate doesn't want to be your girlfriend anymore, so don't call her.' That was cruel, but it wasn't unusual — not where I grew up. After a while, you started distrusting girls and later women. I know women get hurt too. But men are more fragile than they appear. They remember."

Another male manager provided additional support by saying, "I don't think most men are willing to admit the degree to which women are a threat. If a man criticizes or beats you, that's one thing. But when a woman does it, you're more humiliated. We're talking emotional reactions here. Men know women are equally competent on a rational level, but they don't want to deal with it on an emotional level."

As these men spoke, I was reminded of a conversation I'd had some weeks earlier with a male colleague. Walking across campus to an executive education program we were to deliver together, the conversation turned to racquetball. He had just won a game. I told him I hadn't played in a while. Before I could utter another word, he said, "I'd challenge you to a game, but you might win." I told him that was not likely given that I hadn't played in two years. "Nevertheless," he said, "can't do it. It's bad enough when one of the guys beats me, I don't want to suffer the grief I'd get if you won." Losing to a woman on the racquetball court was frightening to this man. When I ran this story past a male business associate of mine who is a successful real estate lawyer, I half expected he would say, "That guy needs help." Instead he said, "I can see his point. I wouldn't want to play racquetball with you either. Men don't like to lose to women. I should know. I'm one of them."

As a rule, women are aware of and fearful of men's discomfort with their competence. At a Daily News Conference where I was a speaker, a female sales manager raised her hand. In response to my comments on the hesitancy of women to speak up when they disagree with male peers and bosses, she said, "I used to think that they really wanted me to debate the issues with them, to play the devil's advocate, but more often than not, they don't. If I have recommendations that might make prior practices look questionable, they want to hear about them in private. At first I thought this was just a company culture thing, but it's not. They criticize each other in public and debate. With me, it's different. I have to introduce my thoughts gently or they ignore me. No one wants a woman to make him look bad."

Women who come into jobs hoping to prove themselves worthy of promotion are the ones most likely to inadvertently make one or more men look bad. Focused on getting ahead, they don't notice the havoc created by their abilities. It's a double bind for women. Male colleagues tell women, "We're the best, and we expect the best. It won't be easy for you. You'll have to work long and hard." When the new female recruit does exactly as advised, she jeopardizes relationships with those around her who consider her "overly gung ho" or a "pitbull."

This, too, is a dysfunctional communication pattern. Not all DCPs are conversations. Some, like this one, are long-term ways of relating to each other. Men tell women that they will have to be the best in order to keep up with them. But they are expected to do so quietly. They are not supposed to disagree. If they do, they risk retaliation because, in many cases, a disagreeing woman is a threat. In the not-so-distant past, women had little to say publicly about work. Now they do. And in many cases, it reminds men that their territory is being encroached upon by people who shouldn't know more than they do.

In 1983 Eugene Koprowski turned to mythology for his *Organizational Dynamics* article prediction that there would be considerable "footdragging and resistance on the part of the male power structure" in the quest for female social equity at work. He explained that "historically, men have developed very ambivalent feelings toward women and the powerful elements in nature that they symbolize. Men currently hold the upper hand in terms of power in our society, and they are not likely to relinquish that power to women without a struggle."[5]

The basis for male ambivalence comes, Koprowski argued, from long-held views of women.

While the status of women in myths suggests they have historically held a secondary role, the symbolic value of women in myths suggests that they have been historically feared as well as desired and possessed by men. Jung, who spent much of his professional career studying the psychological meaning of symbols and myths, suggests that women through the ages have come to symbolize the following: maternal solicitude and sympathy; magic authority; wisdom and spiritual exaltation that transcends reason; helpful instinct or impulse; all that is benign; all that cherishes and sustains; all that fosters growth and fertility; magic transformation and rebirth; the underworld and its inhabitants; anything that is secret, hidden, dark; the abyss; the world of the dead; anything that devours, seduces, and poisons or that is terrifying and inescapable like fate or death.[6]

If Jung was correct, that men respond to women not only as people but as symbols, men are both attracted to and fearful of them. The fear is increased at work, where the presence of women as equals or bosses is relatively new. There are those who will say that this is a lot of nonsense. But such nonsense is at the heart of the subtle stuff women trip over on their path to the top. Women know that one way to elicit fear and retaliation is to challenge men who still have one foot, or two, squarely entrenched in historical symbols of femininity.

Ann Wilk, a forty-five-year-old insurance company senior vice president, has a solution. "I do a lot of behind-the-scenes discussions of ideas," she says. "Rather than surprise men with an idea that they may not agree with, I talk to them before the meeting. Two benefits come from this approach: I learn the weaknesses and strengths of my idea and, when the idea is good, I gain support for it prior to the meeting."

I've shared Wilk's approach with other women. Some think it is too demure. "Why should a woman have to go behind the scenes to sell her ideas?" is one reasonable question. If a woman cannot express herself without fear of retaliation, then she isn't really equal to men, is what some women think when they consider the behind-the-scenes approach. As with most strategies for changing DCPs, some are more comfortable than others. Most women who make it as far as Ann Wilk has do so because they save their major thunder for situations that count.

Another approach is to let the person most likely to disagree know that you expect him to be disappointed in your decision to oppose him but that you must do so for reasons that you then describe. The following example was taken from a conversation between a female and a male computer products manager. The male manager had proposed a strategy for expediting product launches. The female manager, Elise, had some reservations.

> *Elise:* You may find what I have to say unsettling, Jeff, but I can't support this proposal. It doesn't address the role outside vendors play and the slow-ups we have working with our own subsidiaries. If there is a way to address those, I'm open to it.

The success of this approach depends to a large extent on the corporate culture and the relationship between the two people involved. Elise spoke with conviction and avoided personalizing this issue by saying "this proposal" rather than "your proposal." She laid out objective criteria for judging the proposal and expressed willingness to reconsider if her concerns were met. It worked. Jeff took her comments as they were intended and entered into a discussion with Elise about outside vendor and subsidiary challenges.

If Elise had been subordinate to Jeff, her approach might have been different. If men do not like being corrected or challenged by women who are their equals, they like it even less when the woman is a subordinate. As Felice Schwartz wrote in her book *Breaking with Tradition:* "Women know from their first entrance into the gleaming headquarters of the Company that although male senior managers pay public tribute to the need for women in the work force, their underlying feelings are more ambivalent."[7]

For many men, lurking beneath the surface rhetoric is a readiness to treat a female subordinate's disagreement as an indication of ingratitude for the acceptance they and the company have shown by letting her take a management position. There is still a perception that men are "letting" women into companies. It is an antiquated notion but one with a considerable afterlife.

With a boss who thinks like this, Elise should word her response in a nonpersonal manner and speak with conviction while avoiding the impression that she has disregarded the status difference between herself and her boss:

Elise: We need to get this project on the road, Jeff, but it is in the interests of the company to consider outside vendor buy-in and slow-ups at subsidiaries. If we ignore those, we destine this project to failure.

Here Elise is using the company's interests as a frame for her position. She says "we" rather than "I," suggesting a team concern. She recognizes the need to get the project on the road, but implies that speed, while important, is secondary to a comprehensive, potentially successful plan. She is speaking in business language and doing so with conviction in a manner likely to avoid personal affront.

A second alternative is for Elise to skip the idea that the boss is missing the point and offer assistance in making his idea work:

Elise: In order to make this a foolproof plan we'll need vendor buy-in and subsidiary support. I'd be glad to take that on with some help, Jeff.

Elise has moved to the solution rather than introducing the problem. Instead of asking for permission to help out, she has offered to take charge of a team to solve the problem. He may choose to deny her offer. If he does, she hasn't lost anything. If he accepts her offer, she has turned what could have been construed as criticism into an opportunity to work more closely with Jeff on an issue important to him.

Another option is the "cease-to-care" approach. Here the decision to disagree with a male superior or peer is made with full knowledge that he might not like it. Most women find this difficult. They manage their language to avoid personal affront and conflict. They sense what research confirms: although aggressive behaviors may be perceived as more competent, they are less likable.[8] What women often fail to recognize is that men come to expect them to tiptoe around important issues. But they also wonder if the tiptoer has anything substantive to offer.

Lisa Hill Fenning, a U.S. Bankruptcy Judge, concurs. "Female lawyers often want to be liked," she says. "Respect and some fear is usually more effective. There's a mismatch of expectations for women. Men tend to look outside the workplace for emotional support. Women still believe they can get support at work if they do a good job. I'm not advocating dislike. You don't need to make enemies, but you don't need to constantly seek approval either. Trying to give everyone what they want is a subordinate, supportive role. Do this enough and male partners can't envision you as a potential equal who can make competent decisions."

Worrying too much about men being offended is dysfunctional. Besides, many of the senior women I meet have come to the conclusion that women overestimate the extent to which men devote time to considering their own communication styles and those of others. Clara Ferris of Hewlett-Packard believes that women forget that most men don't notice all the subtle nuances of language that women fear they'll find offensive. "Words have more levels of meaning for women than they do for men," says Ferris. "Women read into things and wonder what men meant. They discuss the possibilities and imagine that men do the same. They don't. Men are straighter, more direct. Women have learned to watch carefully how they phrase things. They agonize over words and they think men do too."

What women see as the subtle meanings of words, which they manage carefully to avoid affront, are often not received as such by men. Agonizing over how a male peer or boss might take something can be counterproductive. While the woman is worrying, men are stepping up and being heard. In such circumstances, it is better to be heard too, even if it means saying, "Please excuse the following absence of eloquence, but this plan is on a fast track to nowhere without vendor support and subsidiary buy-in."

PATRONIZING DCPS

Women find themselves left out of important decisions quite frequently. Then they are told, "Don't worry about it" or "It was nothing personal. We just had to make a decision." Time and again they are given the impression that their contributions are secondary; their opinions afterthoughts. Patronizing behaviors deny the value of women's contributions.

Before discussing ways to prevent and terminate patronizing behavior, it's important to note the role women often play in perpetuating it. Research indicates that differences in nonverbal behaviors occur not only as a function of the sex of the person but a function of the sex of those around that person. For example, women tend to smile less in the presence of women than in the presence of men. Women are more likely to behave in "in-role" or stereotypical ways when they are with men. Whether men have more latitude is not known. But anecdotal evidence suggests that they also rely more on "in-role" stereotypically male modes of conduct when in the presence of women.

In her educator role at a top office products company, Clara Ferris shares with women what she sees as a tendency for men to relate to women as wives, mothers, or daughters. "Colleague is a hard category for many men to apply to women. Men become paternal, flirtatious, or dependent in the presence of women. They convey expectations to women by acting in these ways." But Ferris warns, "Women often respond to such expectations without thinking. Women find father figures, knights, big brothers, and confessors in men. Their language expresses this. When they do this, women mess up men's heads too." What Ferris has identified is the reciprocal nature of any pattern. It is always important to ask: Am I contributing to the recurrence of this way of relating? If the answer is affirmative, the first step is to change your own behaviors.

The following conversation is an example of a patronizing DCP.

Kelly: The meeting time you're suggesting isn't going to work for me.
Edward: We have to schedule it then.
Kelly: Why?
Edward: Listen, Kelly, everybody knows you have a lot of outside demands with your family, so if you miss the meeting it won't be a problem.
Kelly: My family has nothing to do with this.
Edward: You know, you look stressed and tired.
Kelly: My fatigue level is irrelevant.
Edward: I think it would be better if we talk about this after you've rested up.

A close look at Kelly and Edward's conversation reveals how women end up frustrated by patronizing DCPs. Edward is pressing his agenda without regard for Kelly's input. In fact, he is rejecting her input since, he explains, it comes from a person with too many family demands and a high stress and fatigue level. Unfortunately, Kelly defends her family involvement, fatigue level, and stress level. She tries to get Edward back on track, but he resists. In her efforts to revise his image of her, she neglects to notice that what he said is inappropriate and unworthy of a cordial reply. By continuously using one-down defense moves (↓) Kelly is yielding control of the interchange to Edward. She is letting him play the knowledgeable big brother or dad and contributing to a way of relating that is dysfunctional.

In hindsight, one of Kelly's options was to direct the conversation back to a nonpersonal track. The following is an example.

> *Kelly:* That meeting time won't work for me.
> *Edward:* We have to schedule it then.
> *Kelly:* Why?
> *Edward:* Listen, Kelly, everybody knows you have a lot of outside demands with your family, so if you miss the meeting it won't be a problem.
> *Kelly:* Your concern for my family is noted, Edward, but let's stick with the subject of the meeting time. I have my calendar here. I see you have yours.

This is abrupt. But it gets the conversation back onto a business track. It is better than Kelly allowing Edward to define her personal life as a reason for not attending a meeting she clearly wishes to attend. At least this approach cuts off the personal aspect of the prior interaction and gets Kelly out of a defensive stance.

Patronizing can also center on work ability. Catalyst, a New York–based research organization devoted to women's business issues, conducted a study focused on female engineers in thirty corporations. One of their conclusions was that communication becomes very important at senior levels. As one female engineer explained,

> Once you've gotten past the second or third level of management . . . even for men, that's the level where things may be based more on the comfort factor and on whether you went to the same school, whether you have a Mason's ring on, than it is based on your technical expertise. They feel if you've reached that level already you've got to be technically qualified. So that's the point at

which your management skills and your style have to meld better with the people you're working with — it becomes more important than your technical skills — that's the point at which I think women experience greater problems.[9]

This same study indicates that women face a "double-edged sword" when they attempt to meld with men by communicating like them. An authoritative management style is viewed negatively in women, yet a more humanistic, participatory style is not respected. Women engineers in this study advised other women to "smile a lot" to avoid offending men.[10] This may avoid offense, but it sends the message that the smiler is not angry — a green light to continue patronizing her.

In most cases, the best response to patronizing communication is a refusal to honor it. This means being unwilling even to talk about personal matters and refusing to allow pats on the back and hugs to hide the fact that someone is not listening and not caring about your input. The emotion must fit the seriousness of the situation. Quips about motherly duties and family obligations must be nipped in the bud. Consider the experience of a female high-technology manager:

"Before I started a new assignment my boss said, 'Oh, by the way, I want you to know that you've got a couple of trips coming up. I thought I should let you know so you could cook up some meals and freeze them.' I just started laughing, and told him that my husband does eighty percent of our cooking and grocery shopping. After a while you learn how to deal with those kinds of comments, but there is no way that would have ever been said to a man coming into a job."[11]

Rather than laugh and explain her husband's duties, why not say what she is thinking: "You wouldn't say that to a man, would you, Will?"

Some women consider demure, pleasant reactions to patronizing remarks as a way of "rolling with the punches." They are rolling themselves right out of senior management. A consulting firm associate believes sometimes you have to be direct if the comment is condescending. One recommendation: "I'm letting that comment pass this time." A less abrupt alternative is "You buy the tickets, Frank, I'll take care of my family's menu." If he cares, he'll give it some thought. If he doesn't, at least you know where you stand and you haven't affirmed it by letting another DCP slip by.

Pregnant and Patronized

The time when women feel most patronized is during pregnancy. In 1993 pregnancy-related complaints to the Equal Employment Opportunity Commission reached a six-year high, which the *Wall Street Journal* described as "reflecting the impact of widespread layoffs and mounting workplace tension over sex roles."[12] The popular trend of downsizing even when companies are profitable has magnified the impact of pregnancy. Add to this the increasing number of women becoming pregnant in their late thirties and early forties and the fact that the salaries of many of these women are equal to or above those of spouses. The result is comments like the one I received recently from a program director whose college-aged children, he admits, were principally raised by their mothers: "I know I'm not supposed to say this, but pregnant women are getting to be a real problem for us. Each time one of them gets pregnant, the whole program is upset."

I heard this same sentiment expressed one week later in a different department of the same company. Closer scrutiny revealed that the source of these directors' problem was not so much pregnant women as penny-pinching superiors expecting them to get by without hiring temporary help during the pregnant women's leave. They were focusing their antagonism in the wrong direction. The woman was the easier target.

Such attitudes toward pregnant women enter into workplace communication. Even if the woman keeps her job, the communication climate she experiences during and after pregnancy is different from any she had previously known.

"I did everything to hide it," Miranda Simonson, regional manager for a Los Angeles–based mid-sized company, explained. "But I gained a lot of weight and my stomach entered the room long before I did. Back then there were more men in the company. They talked to me differently after my pregnancy became visible. I felt like all the work I'd done to build my credibility went out the window. They treated me like I was barefoot and pregnant. My body told them my brain wasn't working anymore. And even after the baby was born, I couldn't regain the credibility I'd lost. My body and my life had become public domain. People came in to ask me questions that weren't their business. Everyone was so focused on my condition that they forgot to notice that my brain was still intact."

Even those women who breeze through pregnancy without illness find that their credibility is compromised. "You look like a boat. There are a few dresses that look good, but not many," a working mother with a newborn told me. "But worse than that, men talk to you in silly ways. They say things like 'You're glowing now,' which is supposed to mean pregnancy suits me. Or they start planning my life after the baby's birth — 'You won't want that assignment. It means some travel. We'll give it to Jim.' The irony is that Jim has three little kids. He doesn't want to be away from home."

Miranda Simonson doesn't view the way men treat you when you're pregnant as just a product of forgetting to think about what they say. "To me it's sabotage," she says. "People are so busy validating their own weaknesses, they are pleased to consider someone's ability compromised. They write you off as if all the work you did was for nothing. It leaves more room for them. They also say things like 'You don't really expect to work full time?' or 'Who will take care of the baby?' None of these things are any of their business. It's just a way to make women feel guilty. None of the men have to listen to that stuff when they become fathers. So why should I?"

Combining career and baby is certainly demanding. But not half as demanding as dealing with thoughtless comments about maternal demands. Children can make their very accomplished adult parents feel insecure. When little people are depending on you, all the advanced degrees and impressive credentials in the world are often insufficient to assure you that you're doing right by them. Child rearing is filled with questions: Am I feeding them well? Have I encouraged them enough? Do they know how much I love them? Under such circumstances "cheap shots" and uninvited advice can cause considerable harm.

One of my male colleagues is the father of triplet toddlers. He is very involved with them. But he readily admits that people do not treat him as any less committed to his job. They don't act as if his brain is functioning less efficiently, although he'll also admit that he is balancing a lot of details. He believes that "it's just different if you're a woman. To many people, women aren't the same after children. It's ridiculous but true."

The long-term solution to this problem is enlightened companies viewing family as the responsibility of both men and women. This could be a long wait. Until division-of-labor stereotypes become more balanced, women must decide whether they wish to contribute to DCPs that undermine their career goals. The following patronizing DCP is a case in point.

> *Steve:* Boy, it must be difficult for you to work and raise your child too.
> *Mary:* It's a challenge at times.
> *Steve:* A while back my wife and I decided we wouldn't pass the responsibility of raising our children on to strangers.
> *Mary:* We haven't done that.
> *Steve:* Oh, of course you haven't. I didn't mean to imply that you aren't a good mother.
> *Mary:* Mark and I share the responsibility and it works out.
> *Steve:* Sue and I share a lot too, but she is at home with the children so both of us can focus on what we need to do.

This conversation places Mary in the position of defending her decision to work. It elicits guilt and implies that doing well means being able to totally focus on home and family. In the first place, Mary's child-care decisions are not Steve's business. To discuss them with him, especially after he has implied that strangers bring up the children of working mothers, gives Steve the impression that it is okay to make derogatory comments about a woman's career/family decisions. Mary's reactions are defensive — "We haven't done that" — or explanatory/defensive — "Mark and I share the responsibility and it works out." She could have avoided this interaction by responding to Steve's comment about the decision he and his wife made with "I have to run to a meeting" or "Best of luck with that decision, Steve. See you later."

These comments cut off further discussion. Impolite? Perhaps. But he isn't exactly Mr. Etiquette. For Mary, the important thing is to exit the conversation or say something that brings the discussion to an early termination. If she wants him to know that she considers his comments insulting, she might try silence as a response to his comment about children being raised by strangers. Or she might say, "I don't see it that way, Steve. But this is no time to discuss child-rearing practices." This last option is useful because it lets Steve know that she does not agree with him. It dismisses the interaction as inappropriate. It does not attack Steve on a personal level. If Steve is educable, some benefits might accrue from encouraging him to consider the appropriateness of his comments.

Patronizing patterns of communication survive as long as there are willing participants available. Whether they are about children, work commitment, loyalty, capacity to lead, or absence of "real experiences," they do little other than place the female participant in a defensive or apologetic posture. Neither is beneficial to her career.

EXCLUSIONARY DCPS

In the course of my interviews with senior executives for this book, a CEO told me in confidence that there is a solution to "the problem of women working with men." He explained, "The answer is to have two standards of communication: one used when women are present and one when they're not. When I was younger, that is what we had. When you were in the presence of women, you knew not to say certain things. You didn't swear or make off-color remarks. You didn't comment on women unless it was to praise their looks or clothes. You treated them with what we thought was respect. Now things are all jumbled up. But we still need two standards. When you're with men, you can let loose. With women you have to be more careful."

As I explained to this CEO, the double-standard approach is destined to failure. Most women do not like double standards and they are not blind to them. A female senior marketing director for a major toy manufacturer had an experience that was still infuriating her when she told me about it. "The other day the CEO was describing some new plans at a directors meeting. He got annoyed with some idea and started swearing. Two seconds into his tirade, he turned to me and said, 'I'm sorry, Sue.' I looked around. Everyone was looking at me. He hadn't apologized to any of them. Why to me? All that does is separate me out. I didn't care for it one bit," she said.

Women consider this kind of treatment a form of exclusion from the club. It underscores that they are not entirely one of the group. Even those who believe the person doing it is attempting to be polite don't care for it. Many women reject the polite theory. The female marketing director believes that "they do it to remind you and everyone there that you are not 'in' and that your presence shouldn't delude anyone into thinking that you are."

Another reason for rejecting the double-standard approach is that in all likelihood one of the standards will be considered superior to the other. Usually it is the male one. Double standards, even ones that seem to address difficulties, perpetuate inequities. Treating women differently from men, rather than trying to address similarities and differences, only serves to perpetuate the discomfort men often feel when women are around. The double-standard answer is too simplistic a solution for a complex problem.

Exclusion takes many forms — physical and verbal. Women are excluded physically or verbally from important interactions. A female law partner of a prestigious New York–based law firm told me of a situation where two male lawyers were discussing aloud their plans to arrange a gathering with important clients. Two other male lawyers and two female lawyers were in the room. "The male lawyers planning the client gathering invited the male lawyers along. Nothing was said to the females. The expenses were being covered by the firm. The two female lawyers came to my office to complain. They had clearly been excluded from an important event. I went straight to the most senior partner, explained the matter, and told him this kind of thing has to stop. We've been losing female lawyers left and right and they're still pulling this stuff."

At another law firm, a female partner confided to me what she described as the ultimate environment of exclusion: "There is one barrier we'll never break through and that is the men's room door. When you pee next to someone, it has a certain bonding effect. Status lines break down at the urinals."

I've studied the exclusion of women in various types of organizations. Much of it is neither purposeful nor vengeful on the part of men. Instead men have grown up with what Erving Goffman, author of *Interaction Ritual,* terms "involvement rules." According to Goffman, expectations regarding involvement are learned and conventional. They vary across cultures. They also vary across genders. On a less-than-conscious level, men simply do not believe women warrant the same level of involvement as men. Women pose what Goffman refers to as subordinate rather than dominant involvement demands.[13]

Men have learned to tune out the words of women because women are usually considered peripheral to the "dominating activity" at hand. What women have to say is assumed to be of less value because women have historically been excluded from important nondomestic decisions. In many companies, women who reach the top are ones whose competence is beyond question. They are women who leave no doubt that they can make it in a man's league.

Prior to making a dinner presentation at a company launching a diversity program, I was introduced by the CFO. In his remarks he praised the group and discussed at some length the company's commitment to promote women despite their admitted less-than-impressive track record in that area. As he was completing his remarks, an idea came to his mind. "I just thought of something," he said, eyes wide and smiling with discovery. He added words to this effect: "There is a woman who should be here tonight. She should be on our diversity team. She represents what we're looking for. Alison Cray is a manager in our European office. Now there is someone women can look to as a role model. Alison has a Ph.D. in physics, she is an accomplished pianist and violinist. She made the Olympic pretrials as an equestrian and has won numerous skiing championships. She should be here, she'd be perfect."

I watched as the women around the table looked down at their napkins, reached quickly to sip from their glasses, exchanged furtive glances, or rolled their eyes. "She sounded perfect all right," one of them later said to me. "Apparently that is what they're looking for. Any females who don't measure up to Ph.D. Olympians, playing concert violin when not conducting physics experiments, winning equestrian medals, or skiing down death-defying slopes aren't senior management material. Do you believe he said that at a diversity meeting? What planet is he on?"

Often diversity committee members are selected by men who think this way. Poorly devised diversity committees are worse than none at all. In such environments women either express anger or remain silent. The ones who do the former often leave. Those who do the latter eventually give up any ambition to succeed or leave. This is a waste of time and talent. If a woman is being excluded, what does she have to lose by bringing it to the attention of the excluder? She is already being left out. She might as well take the initiative to speak up for herself. If the excluder isn't responsive, it's time to be less responsive to his needs. It may be necessary to spell that out for him too. "I'd be glad to help with that, Phil. And I'd be glad to be at the top of the list for the Parker project. Is it a deal?"

A male colleague of mine turns nearly everything he does for people into a deal. I've cringed at times listening to him get a payback for what I considered a minor favor. But he has done well for himself. He may overdo it at times. No one likes to be indebted to someone for the loan of a pencil. But there is something to be said for assuring that you are included in important events.

When exclusion is purposeful, the task of inserting oneself into important events is more difficult. Kate Watson, marketing manager for the research division of a top office products company, found that it was easy for her to be excluded from important international trips to meet major customers. "If I complained, it went in one ear and out the other. One of my colleagues suggested a different approach. He advised me to assume I will be included in the trip. He suggested that I stop by my boss's office a few months before the trip with my calendar in hand. Then I should say, 'Bill, when is that trip to Japan? I want to clear my calendar in advance.' It worked."

This is a case of nipping an Exclusionary DCP in the bud before it happens again. Rather than address the problem in a way that men may interpret as female "whining," it is sometimes better just to assume that you are included, plan on it, make the arrangements, and let them go to the trouble of explicitly excluding you. Then their actions are not deniable. They cannot be attributed to forgetting or a minor oversight.

UNDERMINING DCPS

Coping with challenges at work becomes much more difficult when experts and the media impose even more labels or create fictitious conflicts. Articles about women going home again or society crumbling because selfish women are working are a staple of the popular press. The foundation of these articles is, of course, pure fiction, as was the case with the news reports that Susan Faludi, author of *Backlash,* attacked for creating images of a "man shortage," which raised an unwarranted concern among young women, and "women's burnout," which convinced many that the best place for women is at home baking cookies. These are what mass media experts refer to as pseudo-events. They exist only because the media created them.[14]

The damage such fictions cause is even greater when the source is someone who is usually on your side. Felice Schwartz launched the working world into a frenzy with her 1989 *Harvard Business Review* article "Management Women and the New Facts of Life." Schwartz divided women into "career-primary" and "career-and-family." She advised companies to recognize the former early and "clear artificial barriers from their path to the top." For the majority of women, the "career-and-family" type (later dubbed the "mommy track"), Schwartz recommended that companies provide support but exclude them from the "major players" category used for "career-primary" women.[15]

Dividing women into two groups, those who intend to have or already have children and those who do not, angered women. *Harvard Business Review* published pages of furious responses to Schwartz's article. Schwartz had given men a reason for excluding women and a label to use along with it. Women's efforts were undermined by one of their own.

Schwartz thinks that she was misinterpreted. And she often was. Her article was, in many respects, supportive of women. In her book *Breaking with Tradition* she wrote:

> I realized then that there was a deeper level, too, in women's reactions to my article. In addition to this insistence on my maintaining the conspiracy of silence, because of their basic doubt of employers' motives, women projected onto me their own vulnerabilities and angers, their frustrations, their sense of inadequacy. It took some time to sort out why and how, and I don't know that I have it even now. But here are some thoughts on the complexity of the reaction.
> I touched a nerve in women's feelings about themselves.

Women themselves feel conflicted about whether they do indeed have the commitment to make it to "the top," whatever that entails. It was more palatable for them to blame me or business for having to make trade-offs than to admit to themselves the necessity for doing so.[16]

This is a plausible explanation. Women often are ambivalent about family/work demands. And there was probably some projection. Indeed, Schwartz had touched a nerve in their feelings about themselves. But men are increasingly experiencing similar ambivalence. Consider, for example, the comments of a leading Washington, D.C., attorney, father of two adolescent boys: "I realized a few years ago that I have to be home more. The boys are growing up so fast. I'm afraid I'll turn around someday and they'll be grown. I won't have spent enough time with them. There's a song about that. Every time I hear it I think about how much I've missed. I'm still on the road a lot, but not as much as I used to be. I make sure I'm there when they need me. I want to be there."

Felice Schwartz deserves credit for helping to break a conspiracy of silence — the unwillingness or inability of women to address issues surrounding women and work. But the following comments from her book contradict that contribution and help to undermine women's attempts to combine work and family:

The woman, for example, who is dedicated to her career and is willing to have other people care for her children, who internally remains ambivalent about her choices, doesn't want to be reminded that she is not actively participating in her children's lives because that means to her that she's not a "good" mother. I saw this in a phone conversation I had with a woman who called me in a rage. She told me she had for many years admired me and applauded Catalyst's work, but she hated me now and was deeply resentful of my position. I had accused her, she said, of not caring for her child, of not being a mother to her daughter. She had both a high-powered career and a two-year-old child. I can only assume that my reference to women with children who choose to pursue their careers intensely and are willing to delegate the primary care of their children to surrogates had triggered in her feelings of dissatisfaction and guilt.[17]

Here, Schwartz does not get it. She does not see that, for all the good she has wrought with her word processor, describing a working mother as someone who necessarily delegates her children's "primary care" to a "surrogate" is insulting. It is also inaccurate. The primary care of a child is not changing diapers and baby-sitting, it is loving, instilling values, guiding, playing, and caring.

Schwartz is correct in her sentiment that there are "downsides to women's issues" and it is important to acknowledge them. But dividing women into good and bad mommies, those who care about work and those who care about home, is destructive. It ignores the role and obligations of the father and the societal role companies should play in providing their people with reasonable ways of working. And worse, it undermines women's efforts to succeed in their careers.

The *Wall Street Journal* followed suit in 1993 with an article about the "mommy wars." A front-page piece entitled "Stay-at-Home Moms Are Fashionable Again in Many Communities — Former Professional Women Bring Competitive Edge to Bake Sale, the PTA" described a fictional "battle" between women who work and those who stay at home. Some excerpts:

> A surprising victor is emerging in the Mommy Wars, that ongoing battle between those who work outside the home and those who don't. In pockets of middle- and upper-middle-class America like this one, the stay-at-home mom is fast becoming the newest status symbol of the conscientious 1990s.

> Today, with more than 57% of women in the work force, stay-at-home motherhood is becoming fashionable again in some circles partly because it is a luxury that so few families can afford — the equivalent of, say, a BMW a decade ago.[18]

The article described "stay-at-home" mothers who are rarely home. These, the *Wall Street Journal* dubbed "Power Moms." Such women raise funds for charities. They have car phones and carry date books. These women work but they do so as nonpaid volunteers. They too are away from home.[19]

There are no Power Moms, just as there are no Superwomen. The article referred to a Yankelovich research study indicating that the number of women who would quit their jobs if they didn't need the money has increased in the last few years from 38 percent to 56 percent. The implication: Women want to be stay-at-home mommies.[20]

The responses were numerous and not complimentary. On August 23, 1993, the *Wall Street Journal* published eleven letters to the editor critical of the mommy wars piece. My own appeared and read as follows:

> Haven't we been over this before? There is no war between women who work at home and those who work outside the home. Both are too busy. Women are not fighting with one another over the issue of caring for children. The only "maternally correct" thing is the paternally correct thing as well — love and care for your children, share precious time with them, guide and praise them. Women work for the same reasons men do. If 56% of them might quit their jobs, 56% of men would likely do the same. From CEO down, most prefer to work, but they would gladly take more time with their families. The key is to work smart, not long. Like it or not, quantity of work does not equate with quality. Women and men take care of children. Hats off to either if they want to and can be home, temporarily or permanently. But there is no "Mommy War," no "surprising victor."[21]

Other letters criticized the article for media creation, bias in interpretation, focus on wealthy women, and an absence of discussion about the role of fathers and societal responsibility for quality child care.

These types of articles about women are part of an ongoing societal dysfunctional communication pattern. Like all DCPs, they need to be addressed, preferably prevented. They contribute to the quicksand of indifference and disregard women experience at work. As with exclusionary, patronizing, dismissive, and retaliatory DCPs, the solution lies in raising the awareness of both women and men to their existence and learning new ways of talking with and about each other.

The nastiest aspect of these articles is that they are often written by aspiring female journalists. *Business Week* has done the same thing. Among the examples was an attack, written by two women, on Hillary Rodham Clinton for combining her First Lady "ceremonial tasks with policy making" and suggesting she might not be able to take the heat in the kitchen.[22]

There is no reason why women can't criticize other women, but if leading business journals and magazines are relying on women to do so, a disturbing journalistic pattern is emerging. During a business conference dinner conversation, I asked a *Fortune* magazine editor why it is that articles attacking women leaders are so often authored by women. He paused before answering. So I added, "Is my observation correct?" He looked at me, nodded, and said, "None of the men want to be Faludi-ized." He was referring to Susan Faludi's book *Backlash,* in which she accuses many journalists of contributing to the undermining of women's progress. According to this *Fortune* editor, men are not anxious to step into that line of fire from Faludi or any other feminist with a word processor and a following.

Being able to identify and respond effectively to "the subtle stuff" is imperative if women and men are to change the way they interact at work. It is, after all, the day-to-day interactions between people that constitute the communication climate of an organization. Family-friendly programs cannot make up for daily attacks on women's credibility and competence.

Being overlooked, underpaid, dismissed, passed over, ignored, and undermined on a daily basis takes its toll. It accounts, in large part, for the significant number of women leaving traditional organizations to become entrepreneurs.

The next chapter examines the roots of the subtly disparaging, often career-devastating communication that occurs between men and women at work. Underpinning these communication patterns are stereotypes so relentless that over three decades of the modern women's movement have failed to loosen their grasp.

‖ 4 ‖

STEREOTYPES VS. WORTHY DIFFERENCES

STEREOTYPES LIE AT the roots of the patterns we have looked at so far. Stereotypes are perilous to women's careers: Women lack sports experience, so they can't understand teamwork. They are too emotional. They don't make good leaders. The assertive ones are trouble. All of them are dangerous. They aren't sufficiently committed to their work. They don't work well with other women.

When the prices of goods and services do not quickly change with changes in demand, the reason often given in economic circles is the well-known tendency for prices to be "sticky." While women's skillful participation in nondomestic work has changed dramatically over the last several decades, their perceived value — "price" in the marketplace — lags well behind the reality of their performance and potential. The reason is "sticky" stereotypes: images of women that persist long after the reality has changed.

Researchers Arne Kalleberg and Kevin Leicht confirmed that such stereotypes continue to impede women's progress in organizations. They examined the determinants of survival and success among small businesses headed by both men and women. A lack of similar education, different family roles, and lack of networks of business contacts are some of the commonly cited barriers to women's success as entrepreneurs. "As with many 'facts' in the entrepreneurship literature, however," Kalleberg and Leicht point out, "these claims and assumptions have rarely been subjected to empirical testing; very few studies have directly compared the performance of businesses headed by men and women." They did make a comparison and reported the following:

> Our findings sharply challenge the conventional wisdom regarding women's inferiority in entrepreneurship: the women's businesses we studied were no more likely to fail — and were just as successful — as the men's.[1]

Korn/Ferry International, in a study entitled "Decade of the Executive Woman," also contradicts common wisdom about female competence, commitment, and success. Responses from 716 female executives indicated that, over the last decade, women have changed considerably in their ways of work.

Executive women in 1993 were younger than their 1982 counterparts; 69 percent were married versus 49 percent in 1982. While considerably below the 91 percent of married male executives, it shows that women increasingly combine family and high-powered careers. Most of the women surveyed have graduate degrees in business or law. They've worked hard, and they believe decision-making ability and concern for financial results are the most important traits for executive success. Executive women are often risk takers. They are willing to change jobs to get to the top. They don't change jobs for family reasons so much as to gain increased responsibility, greater challenges, company leadership, and higher compensation. When asked to relocate, these women usually do so. Only 14.1 percent of the Korn/Ferry female respondents had refused a relocation — down substantially from 38.6 percent in 1982. Compared to a 1989 sample of male executives, women were less likely to refuse to relocate. They took no more vacation days than their male counterparts (an average of sixteen days).[2]

Clearly, women are changing. But stereotypes plague them. Several respondents in the Korn/Ferry study mentioned "glass walls" keeping women out of line or operations areas known to be quicker paths to senior positions. When asked to name the greatest obstacle they had to overcome to achieve success, despite some decrease over the years the most frequently cited factor both in 1982 and 1993 was "being a woman/sexism."

To what extent do managers see those characteristics needed to succeed as a manager linked to men more than women? In 1970, organizational researcher Virginia Schein found such a link. When this question was studied again in 1985, O. C. Brenner, Joseph Tomkiewicz, and Virginia Schein found that the 420 men and 173 women managers surveyed in nine firms differed significantly in their views of the similarity between women and managers:

> Although the results for women are encouraging for women aspiring to be managers, the results for men are somewhat disquieting. That male managers have not changed their attitudes over the last fifteen years is a message to corporate leaders and legislators as to the importance of maintaining affirmative action pressures. . . . The research shows . . . that although behaviors have changed, the underlying attitudes of male managers have not.[3]

Even in academic institutions (often considered more receptive to women and less prone to adhere to old stereotypes), similar distorted perceptions persist. Economics, for example, was described by the *New York Times* as a field of "subtle exclusion" of women. Women have earned 22 percent of all Ph.D.s in economics over the last decade and they move easily into entry positions, yet women account for only 8 percent of tenured associate professors at eighty universities with graduate-level economics programs. At Stanford University, for example, despite increases in female faculty in recent decades, 43 percent of departments still have no tenured women. In a recent ranking of twenty-one peer universities, including the Ivy League and the Pacific 10, Stanford was nineteenth in the percentage of women on its faculty and seventeenth in the percentage of female full professors. Apparently even the enlightened fall short when it comes to relinquishing antiquated views of female competence.[4]

If men were totally to blame, this book would be easier to write. They aren't, however. The stereotypes about women's commitment to work, ability to lead, emotionality, readiness to cause trouble, and inability to work with each other linger because efforts to disable them have not been sufficiently pervasive or appreciative of the tenacity of gender impressions. Women, perhaps lulled by the initial gains of the women's movement in the 1960s and 1970s, underestimated the effort it would take to change organizational cultures to accommodate and value women. Most of us thought that proving ourselves capable through education and hard work would be enough. Cohesive in the early years of this movement, women in the 1980s seemed to distance themselves from each other, perhaps following the great American tradition of rugged individualism. They soon found that they were reaching senior levels much more slowly than they'd hoped, or not at all. With few women in positions of leadership, stereotypes were still in place.

Since closed minds can attribute small numbers of successful women to aberration, the exception does not negate the stereotype, but strengthens it. If she weren't different, the reasoning goes, wouldn't many more women have accompanied her to the top? Small numbers of women cannot influence the communication climates of companies either. They must accommodate or risk rejection.

Fear is another reason for the endurance of inaccurate stereotypes about women. In an era when women have supposedly gained equality, many report that to avoid threatening men they are careful not to sit next to other women at work meetings. Many women in business share what amounts to an unspoken agreement to disagree with each other occasionally. They purposely avoid the appearance of being united against men. Only when women are well represented do they relax — and that representation level has been extremely difficult to achieve.

Stereotypes also linger because both the sexes believe that the United States surpasses all other countries in its accommodation of businesswomen. The growing evidence is that the United States — for all its equality measures, laws, and talk of diversity — lags behind many countries considered more traditional and conservative. President Vigdis Finnbogadottir of Iceland told the 1993 Global Forum for Women that her country has been accepting of women's work skills for centuries. Countries, like hers, that historically depended on men to fish depended on women to take leadership roles at home and in the community and government.

Frederica Olivares, president and publisher of Olivares Publishing Company in Milan, Italy, believes that the ability to appreciate gender differences is greater in many European countries than in the United States. Writing in the *Harvard Business Review,* Olivares observed that

> adopting a leadership style that draws upon what is unique to their experience as women is less new and surprising for European observers. The history, culture, and socialization of those countries where a strong family-focused socialization exists (France, Italy, Germany, Spain, for example) or where a vigorous and long-lived women's movement tends to emphasize diversity over conformity (Italy and Germany), make it possible for women in management to retain a gender-conscious style in organizations.[5]

Olivares went on to explain that these are countries where "historical memory" amply records women's economic and managerial savvy as farmers, artisans, and small entrepreneurs. She described this mutual appreciation across genders as a "complementary contribution model based on acceptance and worthy differences." The ability to easily draw upon the riches of both male and female inheritance and experience is, according to Olivares, needed by organizations facing global challenges in the 1990s and beyond.

"Other Nations Elect Women to Lead Them, So Why Doesn't U.S.?" asked the *Wall Street Journal* in a front-page article in 1993. It described how countries considered far more conservative and biased against women than the United States have elected women to leadership. Countries that have elected women as prime ministers or presidents include Western nations (Britain, France, Canada, Ireland, Portugal, Iceland, Norway), Asian nations (the Philippines), Latin American nations (Argentina, Bolivia, Nicaragua), Eastern European nations (Poland), Mideast nations (Israel, Turkey), Asian subcontinent nations (India, Pakistan, Bangladesh, Sri Lanka), and West Indian nations (Haiti, Dutch Antilles, Dominica).[6]

U.S. women have made impressive political gains over the last two decades. The number of women mayors has risen more than tenfold to 175. Women in Congress have nearly doubled to 47 in the House and 7 in the Senate. But most experts believe it will be a long wait before a woman wins the U.S. Presidency, despite an increasingly enlightened electorate.

Many U.S. companies have developed diversity programs in the belief that they would move women forward and establish mutual appreciation and acceptance of "worthy differences." But as Ann Morrison, director of the San Diego Center for Creative Leadership and author of *The New Leaders,* explains, such programs often fall short of their goal:

> The word was not used in human resource circles until a few years ago, but it now pops up regularly in phrases such as "valuing diversity" and "managing diversity." *Diversity* is often viewed as an alternative to *affirmative action,* which has taken on negative connotations because of its association with the government's imposition of "quotas" and failed attempts to integrate the various layers of the American workforce. To make diversity a more innovative and appealing idea, some people are reluctant to define diversity as anything more than an appreciation of differences that may improve an organization's performance. These people are reluctant to include the notion of integration or adequate representation in the definition for fear that diversity will come to be viewed as little more than a new label for affirmative action. Yet any reasonable definition of diversity must include integration itself, not simply an awareness of its value.[7]

The *Wall Street Journal* exposed a number of diversity programs as easy ways for companies to look good on paper while declining to promote women.[8] These "programs" can do more harm than good for women in highly traditional organizations. They emphasize the differences between the sexes, making it tougher for women to overcome stereotypes, and they do not get at the real issues. The woman who helped DuPont institute progressive, women-friendly programs left because women's value remained low. She explained, "We ruled out everything except something which is the most elusive of all — culture." Another woman joined a support group of "fast-track" DuPont women in 1989. All were mothers. Over the next few years she watched as their careers derailed one after the other.[9]

This wouldn't be so surprising had DuPont not been rated as one of the most family-friendly companies in the United States. For some companies, apparently, "family-friendly" has become a way of looking like you're doing something for women while actually only placating a few with family leave. It's far easier to give some women a few weeks of family leave than to promote women in significant numbers throughout an organization.

Even good diversity programs typically ignore the pervasive effects of dysfunctional communication patterns. Treating "attitudes" as the main enemy, they neglect the day-to-day interactions in which stereotypes find expression. The contribution of communication to the devaluation of women is rarely explored. This is the stuff of hostile cultures.

As currently constructed, diversity programs cannot cure the ills that keep women out of senior executive positions until communication itself is evaluated and altered. In fact, diversity programs are harmful to the extent they serve as false indicators of company commitment to women and minorities. They contribute to the shelf life of dangerous stereotypes by serving as a cover for the true feelings of management regarding the promotion of people different from themselves.

No, diversity programs alone are not the answer. Many people running organizations are as appreciative of women as they are likely to get; one more seminar won't tip the balance. Efforts to get at the roots, ferret out the prejudices, and clean up the organizational culture must be individual as well as programmatic, and they must be sophisticated and unrelenting. To borrow a term from Norway's woman prime minister, Dr. Gro Harlem Brundtland, whose country has sought and achieved gender balance in politics, worksites need not be feminized but rather "normalized." When over 50 percent of the workforce is female, normalizing is long overdue.

WHAT TO DO ABOUT STEREOTYPES

Once women and men come to the realization that much remains to be done for women to become equals with men in business, the question remains: What to do? The answer is to recognize damaging stereotypes and related DCPs for what they are, rather than continuously contribute to their existence.

The view that women lack team sports experience and are therefore unsuited to senior management positions is one glaring example of a stereotype that limits women's progress and affects the ways men and women communicate. According to this teamwork fallacy, women can't tolerate competitive pressures because they haven't learned first-hand the rigors of being "team players." They've never played to win with the same intensity as men so, the story goes, their memories lack the agony of defeat and the ecstasy of victory.

The truth is, few women lack sports experience. They have known the agony and the ecstasy. They've experienced the mutual reliance of teamwork and the demands of working together to bring home a victory. It's just that the viewing audience, whether in the arena or watching television, has tended to be smaller. In terms of varsity and professional sports, far more men view from the stands than play on the field. Actually, most men and women spend a good deal more time watching sports than directly participating in them. Should we therefore assume that men somehow derive more genuine sports experience from their spectator positions than women? Yet a belief that women lack the sports experiences of men continues to shape expectations regarding women's leadership potential.

Even for those women who lack extensive team sports experience, the belief that this somehow limits business ability deserves scrutiny. As a forty-five-year-old male senior insurance executive told me, "Sports is an analogy that can be used to rationalize almost anything men do. The truth is, though, that most businesses are run more like the military than like teams. They tell you that you're on a team, but you're really in a platoon. A sports team doesn't have a formal hierarchy. The first baseman doesn't tell the shortstop what to do. If you can't play the sport, no amount of kissing up is going to get you ahead. Who are we kidding with all this sports talk?"

Many women don't lack team experience; they simply don't find it at work. They're told that it's there, but being a "team player" in many businesses has come to mean not disagreeing with the boss and knowing how to "play along to get along."

Sharon Easton, vice president of a northeast financial services company, discovered this when she tried to change the meeting location of the company senior executive retreat. "I complained in writing on an employee satisfaction questionnaire two years in a row about the retreat being held at a country club with a men-only bar. After two more years of being left out of post-retreat bar conversations, I decided to raise the topic in person. I told my immediate superior that it wasn't appropriate to hold an executive retreat at a country club with a bar that excludes women. I reasoned aloud that the company CEO had on several occasions stated that efforts were being made to advance women's careers, to promote them to senior levels. Frankly there were few signs of that, but it had been said. My boss told me, 'Let it drop, Sharon.' I couldn't take that for an answer, so I repeated my protest. 'Listen, Sharon,' he said, 'you are a team player or you're not. It's as simple as that. The CEO belongs to this club. Having the retreat here saves a lot of money. If I were you, I'd just drop the subject.' To be honest, I dropped it. I'm no fool. But I wrote it on my employee satisfaction questionnaire again the next year."

Teamwork is often confused with closing one's eyes to problems and doing what the boss expects. It can mean loyalty to boss and company even when they might cut your job at any moment. In fact, many business teams are more show than reality. They represent what communication researchers Gail Fairhurst and William Sarr call "the illusion of participatory management." People are brought together to "make decisions" when in actuality those decisions have already been made by others or will be made regardless of "team" input.[10]

Women may not lack team sports experiences; the majority merely abhor some of the "team" experiences they encounter at work. Deficient sports experience doesn't keep women out of major decisions at work; what does is the mistaken belief that women lack such experience, and an illusion that teams function in businesses the same way they do in sports.

ONE WOMAN'S EFFORTS

Dismantling poisonous stereotypes and redirecting or terminating dysfunctional patterns of communication is a tough job. Among those who have chosen to do their part to smooth the path for women is Jenifer Morrissey. As an engineer at a leading computer products company, Morrissey saw the contradictions between company policy and day-to-day communication. She observed differential treatment of women that was destructive to their careers. Like so many other women, she participated in DCPs. She experienced fear of retaliation when seen talking with other women in the hallway and she avoided any appearance of uniting with them. Like so many others, she tired of the charade and eventually resigned from her company. Before leaving, however, she wrote a five-page memo describing in a sophisticated, professional, nonaccusatory fashion the climate in which she had worked for ten years and the ways in which it compromised the value of women.[11]

Her memo contained references to DCPs between men and women and descriptions of the stereotypes that support them. She exposed inaccurate perceptions of women as less valuable than men, as less committed, and as causing trouble. Drawing upon her graduate studies, she used literature and research to support her perceptions. She described experiences and interactions that led her to question whether she had chosen the right career — one where she could succeed in the company of people who respected her contributions.

Her memo contained four themes: (1) why I'm leaving; (2) why I'm leaving this division; (3) why I'm leaving (company name); and (4) why I'm leaving engineering.

On page one, Morrissey explained the primary reason for the memo: "Managers have often shared their frustration with me about their organization's inability to retain high-caliber women. Now that I'm one of those women leaving, I want to help those managers and others by explaining the reasons why I'm leaving. I hope that by sharing my experiences, managers and others will become more aware of what causes this retention problem and will then be able to generate solutions."

Morrissey went on to describe in detail the conditions she had experienced, referring for support to readings about women and work. Morrissey cited and agreed with author Patricia O'Brien's observation: "I found that moving up in the system meant you got to be ignored by a much higher class of men."[12] She also referred to a study by Catalyst researchers that found that women must prove themselves before promotion rather than being promoted on potential as is common for men.[13]

With regard to ethics and values, Morrissey described the "Female System" as process oriented. In contrast, the "Male System" is product-goal oriented; the ends justify the means. She explained that women must reform their ideas to be "data-centric" in order to have them appreciated. Morrissey quoted Max DePree's book *Leadership Is an Art* — "Leaders need to foster environments and work processes within which people can develop high-quality relationships with . . . our clients and customers"[14] — as support for her belief that customers deserve attention after a sale because there should be a responsibility to customers with whom relationships are developed. She explained, "I have tried to promote my alternative view but have had only limited success. The lack of success has contributed to my decision to leave."

Morrissey found the attitudes of some of her male co-workers a source of "destructive stress." She wrote, "They have said that they believe their careers are on hold until more women are promoted. I was left with the impression that if I were promoted, I would not be respected by my male peers."

The memo described the extent to which women must remain passive even at senior levels. Morrissey wrote, "I've perceived discomfort in some male co-workers when I have offered leadership assistance or feedback. Since I view this discomfort as a detriment to teamwork, and teamwork is important to me, I've had to modify my approach, becoming more passive." She quoted Catalyst's 1992 study of engineers for support: "The corporate engineering culture is male-oriented, with intense pressure to conform to 'masculine' styles and deny issues of concern to women. In this environment, a competent woman is likely to be considered 'too aggressive.'"[15]

Morrissey recognized within herself and other women a desire to prove themselves without mentors or networks. She explained her revised view: "Only recently have I discovered the value of networking. Through my network contacts, I have learned that my experiences in male-dominated professions are not unique. In fact, having other women in male-dominated professions describe similar experiences has helped me realize that to pursue engineering I've had to give up many things that are important to me. Perhaps if I'd had these network contacts earlier in my career, I might have developed coping techniques that would have helped me thrive in the corporate engineering environment."

Morrissey's departure might have been avoided had her company understood the communication climate she faced on a daily basis. But when I talked with her some months after her departure from the company, she explained, "I wish I had learned how to deal with conflict, how to communicate more effectively on an interpersonal level. My training did not provide that and it is so very important for bridging the differences between how men and women think."

Morrissey is now considering her next career and seems to have few regrets about leaving engineering and her company of ten years. While there, she did hone her leadership and professional skills. For her, a woman in her early thirties, many opportunities lie ahead. But she realizes now that there are interpersonal skills she might have applied to deal with the patterns of male-female communication that fostered her ambivalence about her job and career. She says she wrote her memo in part because she felt a responsibility to women who remain at the company and who might find her departure a reason for reflection on their own potential.

THE COMPLEXITY OF THE TASK AT HAND

Jenifer Morrissey not only had the confidence to consider a career change and move on, she also had the financial stability needed to make such a bold move. In her early thirties with no children, she had a world of options before her. She decided to take some of them.

Departures of female managers are frequent in traditional American businesses. For those women who are interested in becoming entrepreneurs or who would just as soon avoid the hassle of trying to change belligerent, antiquated systems, leaving is the best decision. But what of those many women who decide to stay — the ones for whom the route Morrissey has taken is not an attractive option?

For them the answer must be a willingness to recognize and face the poisonous stereotypes that live below the surface of women's daily work experiences and to change the dysfunctional patterns of communication that emerge and draw their strength from these stereotypes. Memos like Morrissey's are only a beginning.

Reformulating the rules of female-male work communication — verbal and nonverbal — is a complex and difficult task. Women and men operate according to communication rules for their gender, what experts call "gender codes." They learn, for example, to show gratitude, ask for help, take control, and express emotion, deference, and commitment in different ways.

Erving Goffman's 1976 book, *Gender Advertisements,* provides pictorial evidence of rules for the way men and women relate nonverbally to each other. Using hundreds of photos of women and men in advertisements, he showed how women are often presented in positions near the floor, seemingly whining or begging. They pout and, like children, hold a man's hand from behind. They are depicted listening to men talk, or with a bashful knee-bend, looking wide-eyed at a protective or authoritative male. Through these advertisements, Goffman revealed latent rules for looking feminine.[16]

The female models, Goffman tells us, do not seem to consider and decide how to pose; they intuitively know. His observations suggest that women and men slip into ways of appearing in each other's presence that reinforce commonly held expectations.[17] The women depicted in Goffman's work provide a window into what author and researcher Arlie Russell Hochschild describes as "the social quietude of an earlier era."[18] In the 1990s, women choose between competing rules about looking "feminine" and looking "professional."

While Goffman's 1976 work focused on rules for male and female outer appearance, he also described rules that establish a permissible range of behaviors and feeling beyond which a woman is perceived as either too feminine or not feminine enough, and ones that similarly constrain male behaviors. In her review of Goffman, Hochschild points out that women have not yet escaped the ranges of permissible behavior Goffman identified nearly two decades ago. Most women need to feel a positive sense of femininity to feel good about themselves. In attempting to be perceived as a professional in traditional male work settings, women mix old and new codes for behavior, male and female expectations for appearance, feelings, and behavior.

Needing to balance two sets of rules in order to survive and hopefully thrive in what has been a male domain, working women have turned to a number of advice books about dress and strategies for infiltration and acceptance. Some of these books dismiss feminine ways and advocate straight talk and direct dealing. Others, like Sonya Friedman's *Smart Cookies Don't Crumble,*[19] advise that women feel less grateful, since feeling so is a trap. Books like Robin Norwood's *Women*

Who Love Too Much[20] and Colette Dowling's *The Cinderella Complex*[21] suggest that the main problem is traditional female rules, not traditional male rules. Women make themselves unhappy by adhering to old ways of thinking and acting.

More recent writings like Sally Helgesen's *The Female Advantage* suggest that women's communication is actually superior to that of men. Women are advised to strengthen their natural tendencies rather than abandon them. Their greater emotional insight, sensitivity to others, and inclination to be supportive is presented as a viable means of achieving success in today's business world, where hierarchical forms of management are giving way.[22]

Such books train women to manage how they act or how they feel. To Goffman, everyone is an actor. These books, as Hochschild points out, are "acting manuals" for women. Such books are rare for men. While men and women act and abide by surface rules regarding appearance and deeper rules regarding thoughts and feelings, women are doing far more work in this area. This may be in part because they are usually subordinate to men, and subordinates do more conscious monitoring of their actions. But it is also because women's lives have been inexorably changed by the women's movement. They are now expected to achieve in nondomestic ways. They come to this challenge with communication rules unsuited to the task, since what seems feminine is often at odds with what is considered professional and competent. To accommodate, women switch, mix, and balance modes of communication, as Hochschild explains, "to seem 'just so feminine' in one aspect of self in order to seem 'just so masculine' in another."[23]

All of this switching, mixing, and balancing is demanding and generally one-sided. Whether the advice followed is to abandon all traces of femininity or to celebrate it as an advantage, women see themselves as the ones who must strategize. This one-sided process of adaptation has exhausted women in their efforts to be successful at work. There is nothing inherently wrong with books that advise women to change. Without change the likelihood of them succeeding is not great. But the expectation that women alone must change in order to accommodate male ways of acting and feeling is truly problematic. Communication isn't unidirectional. Women may change their ways of acting, but until men also change, dysfunctional patterns of communication will continue.

Jenifer Morrissey's memo, and others like it, are the beginning of a much-needed dialogue between women and men. They point out that male and female work codes differ. They do not claim general advantages for either sex, but rather that both bring important skills and inclinations to work. For men and for women, there is no single style, no simple strategy likely to foster complementarity in male-female communication. Like men, sometimes women must be assertive and even aggressive to be heard. At other times, the greater advantage lies in listening and reasoning.

The challenge women face is not to adapt themselves constantly to male expectations, vacillating endlessly between the feminine and the professional, but finding ways to work with men to revise gender codes and relinquish stereotypes that favor one gender more than the other. Memos may initiate the process, but they cannot bring it into the day-to-day work interactions of men and women. They may expose stereotypes, but they cannot depose them. Only through intervening in dysfunctional communication patterns can women and men learn to work effectively together. The rest of this book is devoted to deposing the negative stereotypes of women and the dysfunctional communication patterns that both prove and perpetuate their existence.

Much work is already under way. "This woman thing is really taking off," one male senior executive told me. He was referring to the increased likelihood of women to demand representation at senior levels and their greater tendency to speak up when offended. Women are undergoing in larger numbers than ever before what Mary Catherine Bateson calls, in her book *Composing a Life*, the "reshaping of identity," a form of skilled reconstruction.[24] Women have difficulty in determining how to communicate their discontent without ruining their chances for advancement. Their relational orientation and fear of derogatory labels discourage confrontational approaches. Jenifer Morrissey sent a memo, but she also left the company and is currently considering her next step. She is fortunate, she explained to me, "that

I have no children and my husband is completely supportive. I can make choices other women cannot."

For many the answer is to leave, to become one's own boss. Women owned 32.2 percent of all sole proprietorships in 1990, up from 23 percent in 1977, according to the Small Business Administration. But for women who are unwilling to take the entrepreneurial track to leadership, the options are either to remain silent and hope for the best or to speak up. More and more women are choosing to speak up. They are refusing to do *all* the reshaping, *all* the relinquishing of old rules. Whether they take an "in your face" approach, abruptly confronting men with their adherence to outmoded stereotypes and expectations or whether they seek to educate themselves and the men with whom they work to gender differences in communication rules, the result can be a long-overdue reconstruction of the communication architecture of the workplace.

‖ 5 ‖

LEADERSHIP: BY WHOSE STANDARDS?

HARVARD PROFESSOR ABRAHAM ZALEZNIK believes that success in business requires "leadership compacts" involving superiors and subordinates doing their utmost to help organizations succeed.

Hero leaders are giving way to an image of leadership as employing power in the service and with the assistance of others. Leaders must, as Warren Bennis has proposed, elicit trust. To do so, Bennis says, leaders must be competent. There must also be congruity between what they say and do. And they should be constant in ensuring people that they are on their side.[1]

In *The Fifth Discipline: The Art and Practice of the Learning Organization*, Peter M. Senge of MIT suggests that leaders are no longer men on horseback who shape up organizations through the force of their personalities. Leaders are now supposed to learn along with subordinates. They are no longer expected to know all the answers but rather to seek the best ones.[2]

Burt Nanus, author of *The Leader's Edge: The Seven Keys to Leadership in a Turbulent World*, considers leaders people who "attract the voluntary commitment of followers, energize them, and transform organizations into new entities with greater potential for survival, growth, and excellence."[3] His later book, *The Visionary Leader*, focuses on the mentoring aspect of leaders necessary to make their vision become reality.[4]

There is nothing within these and other similar definitions of leadership to suggest that leaders must be male. On the contrary, a growing number of experts argue that women are better suited to the new leadership that empowers subordinates. Judith Rosener's research reported in "Ways Women Lead" revealed that men describe themselves in ways that characterize "transactional leaders." They see their jobs as a series of transactions with subordinates in which rewards are exchanged for services. Rosener says that women describe themselves in ways that characterize "transformational leaders." They encourage subordinates to transform their own self-interests into the interests of the group through concern for a broader goal. As Rosener interviewed women leaders she found that they tend to share power and information, encourage participation, enhance other people's self-worth, and get others excited about their work. Employees are allowed to contribute in order to feel powerful and important. In other words, says Rosener, women leaders tend to be "interactive" in their relationships with subordinates.[5]

At the core of "interactive leadership" is inclusion, a characteristic consistent with the new leader definitions at the beginning of this chapter. If women are inclusive and new leaders tend to empower others, motivate, care about their employees, and bring out the best in them, then shouldn't women be running GM right now? Of course, they are not, and what Rosener writes about the limitations of female inclusive leaders may help explain why.

> Like most who are familiar with participatory management, these women are aware that being inclusive also has its disadvantages. Soliciting ideas and information from others takes time, often requires giving up some control, opens the door to criticism, and exposes personal and turf conflicts. In addition, asking for ideas and information can be interpreted as not having answers.[6]

Nancy Nichols, an editor and author for the *Harvard Business Review*, recognized the danger in claiming for women the interpersonal, nurturing, integrative sides of leadership. In her article "Whatever Happened to Rosie the Riveter?" she pointed out the hazard in premature celebration of a female leadership advantage.

Despite the popularity of the idea that women bring something special to the management table, there is also a certain danger inherent in this belief. For even as we seek to define gender roles, we perpetuate our prejudices. If women start to define themselves as good at the soft skills of communications, you better believe that someone will say that the "real" work of managers is number crunching and strategic analysis — things that women, well, just aren't up to. Remember, as soon as Rosie got good at riveting, factory work was all about welding.[7]

Under these conditions, should women trade one set of stereotypes for another and claim that their relational orientation, concern for people, tendency to listen, and supportiveness make them better leaders than men? Most organizations haven't adopted the new leadership definition in practice. Most rule rather than lead, coerce rather than motivate. And no amount of shouting, "Women are more sensitive and better suited to the new types of leadership!" is likely to gain them an edge in such places.

The fact is, women and men must be able to alter their leadership styles to suit the demands of the situation at hand. Sometimes hierarchical leadership is necessary. At other times, tasks are better suited to what researchers Louis Barnes and Mark Kriger of Northwestern describe as "network leadership." Potential leaders should train themselves to adapt to the needs of the organization. This isn't to say they should be schizophrenic, shifting rapidly from one style to another, but they should be prepared to respond to a variety of demands, contexts, and goals. There is no inherent male advantage here. As Barnes and Kriger tell us:

> Effective organizational leadership needs *both* hierarchical and network leadership. We must learn to advocate two seemingly different and sometimes opposite perspectives. The two are hard for one person to assume simultaneously without living a paradox and, at times, advocating almost the opposite of what he or she may represent publicly. It means two very different roles. One endorses and advocates hierarchy. The other builds and supports network leadership.[8]

Barnes and Kriger define one-sided leadership as a "formula for failure." While they accept the arguments of those who define leaders according to traits like charisma, energy, and style, they consider these descriptions insufficient. Managers — senior and junior — are both leaders and followers. The demands of their work require them to approach leadership in a hierarchical, commanding fashion at some times, and in a networking, supportive way at other times.

There is no such thing as a born leader. Leadership is more than a set of static personality traits. Effectiveness depends on an interplay of traits, style, tasks, and expectations of others. In most organizations, therefore, leaders can't afford to be one-sided. As formal hierarchies diminish, leaders must work with many more people. Suppleness in style is becoming imperative.

Women and men can learn to broaden their leadership styles. The challenge women in particular face is how to cope with stereotypes and dysfunctional patterns of communication that accompany different leadership styles. As a society, we are more accepting of directive behaviors from men and supportive behaviors from women. Leadership style flexibility opens new avenues for crossover. It responds to the dilemma most women face in traditional organizations: Do I become one of the boys? No, you must do what is required based on the situation at hand and your own skills and ethics.

LEADERSHIP STYLES

It's important to understand just what flexible leadership style means. What types of leadership are there? What types of situations match with each leadership type? University of Southern California leadership experts Alan Rowe, Warren Bennis, and I developed the Leadership Style Inventory to answer these questions.

The inventory appears below. Follow the directions carefully to derive your own leadership profile. After you've added up each column, you have four scores. The four column scores correspond to four types of leadership style: (1) Commanding, (2) Logical, (3) Inspirational, and (4) Supportive. The chart that follows the inventory describes the characteristics of each style.

People with high Commanding scores (column 1) are the "take charge" type. They want to get things done and expect people to take direction. Logicals (column 2) are more analytical. They persuade

Leadership Style Inventory

© *Alan J. Rowe, Kathleen K. Reardon, and Warren Bennis*
(This form may not be reproduced without written permission)

To score the instrument, use the number 8 for the responses that are MOST like you, a 4 for those that are MODERATELY like you, a 2 for those that are LITTLE like you, and a 1 for the responses that are LEAST like you. Do not repeat any number when answering a given question. You *must* use each of the four numbers when responding to a question. There are no right or wrong answers, so respond with what comes to mind first.

1. I see my role as:	establishing organization's objectives	identifying new directions	making goals exciting	listening to people's concerns
2. I prefer an organization:	that has a strong work ethic	that can easily adapt to change	that values people with new ideas	that encourages cooperation
3. I expect my associates to:	be loyal	be reliable	understand me	be supportive
4. To gain commitment, I	provide incentives	rely on logical arguments	create a feeling of trust	enable people to perform
5. I expect people to:	show initiative	persevere	make a commitment to their work	participate with others
6. Power is used to:	maintain control	achieve objectives	restructure the organization	share responsibility
7. I believe people should:	be self-confident	be logical	have daring ideas	work well with colleagues
8. To improve performance, I	insist on meeting goals	offer challenging assignments	rely on the team approach	assure fair evaluation
9. I look for:	personal status	job fulfillment	dignity and respect	acceptance
10. Change requires:	concrete actions	the right timing	understanding people's needs	a feeling of security
11. Successful people are:	hard driving	competent	creative	effective communicators
12. I value:	authority	professionalism	independence	consensus
13. Others see me as:	committed to my work	being a good problem solver	having broad vision	being a team player
14. I try to be:	concise	thorough	open minded	sensitive
15. Performance depends on:	specific actions	consistent plans	exploiting opportunities	a feeling of trust
16. Organization should:	have well-defined plans	insist on quality output	foster collaboration	build on shared values
17. When there is a problem I:	take charge	explore my options	network with colleagues	consult with friends
18. I admire people who:	are efficient	are flexible	are imaginative	are dependable
19. I constantly try to:	work hard	plan ahead	seek new challenges	learn from others
20. I feel it is important to:	achieve results	be accurate	have high expectations	appreciate others

---

Leadership Styles

Commanding	*Logical*
Focuses on controls	Analyzes new directions
Achieves results	Solves complex problems
Takes charge	Formulates plans
Persuades by directing	Persuades by reasoning
Rapid change	Incremental change
Inspirational	*Supportive*
Envisions new opportunities	Tries for consensus
Introduces radical ideas	Facilitates work
Empowers others	Encourages openness
Persuades by creating trust	Persuades by involving
Radical change	Reactive change

---

other people by walking them through their reasoning. An individual with high scores in both Commanding and Logical is a person who thinks through options and formulates plans, but also expects to get results quickly.

Inspirationals are creative people who empower other people by inviting them to share in their visions. Supportives want to please other people by involving them in decisions and seeking consensus. While it is theoretically possible to have a combined Commanding-Supportive style, we've not found people with this combination in our research. Other combinations are more likely. For example, a Supportive-Logical style would involve a predisposition to reason through alternatives and work with people to assure their buy-in and contentment with the one selected.

Few business executive groups score high on the Supportive dimension. The mean score in our research to date is 53. So if your score is higher than 53, you can consider yourself relatively Supportive by business standards. Means for Commanding, Logical, and Inspirational are 86, 80, and 81, respectively.

Stereotypes of women as more nurturant and caring suggest they should score higher than men on the Supportive dimension. Some do, some don't. Our research does not support the stereotype that women leaders are consistently more supportive. Stereotypes of men as direct and controlling suggest they should score higher on the Commanding dimension than women. Some do, some don't. Using the Leadership Style Inventory we've found that women real estate brokers are less Commanding than male investment bankers, but their job is the reason, not their gender. Male real estate brokers are also less Commanding than investment bankers.

Real estate brokers are expected to persuade and/or inspire. They don't direct people to buy; they encourage them. "I have to be able to do each of these styles," a male real estate broker said after realizing that his scores were spread fairly evenly over the four styles. "There are times when I need to be commanding, but most often I find myself being logical and supportive. My clients want to know what's in it for them, and they want my reassurance too. I can't afford to rely on one style. I have to be able to adapt to the circumstances at hand."

When I administered the leadership inventory to (mostly) male traders on the stock exchange floor of a major L.A.–based bank, most had high Commanding scores. I thought they might be uncomfortable with that, but they weren't. "Are you kidding?" one said to me. "We have to tell people what we think with conviction or they won't listen. No one wants us to equivocate or focus on their feelings rather than the route to results. Nope, we're Commanding all right. And that may be why we don't get along [with each other] all that well."

"Commanding and proud of it" is how the traders described themselves. Most also scored high on the Logical dimension. They needed to be able to explain and reason through their choices, but do it quickly and with conviction about their advice. Their general consensus: Most clients don't need to like you. They want to understand quickly why you're giving them advice, and then they want you to move on it. As one trading expert explained, "A lot of money is involved and time is of the essence. They know you can't fool around making them feel cozy."

Judy Rosener's finding that women tend to be more inclusive than men in their leadership style can be explained by the Leadership Style Inventory (LSI). Rosener's study involved "prominent women leaders." Most had reached a point in their careers where the desire to be inclusive could be implemented without serious repercussions. For women who are not yet prominent leaders, the risk can be greater. So what should a woman inclined to inclusiveness do? Should she take on more transactional ways of leading? Should she be true to herself and do as she pleases? In all likelihood, neither is the best route. Some tasks and situations lend themselves to inclusiveness. When these situations arise, being able to empower and motivate others is a tremendous asset. Other kinds of tasks and situations call for immediate action, decisiveness, and a willingness to exclude people whom you would otherwise include. Leadership, whether male or female, requires knowing the difference. A woman whose style is consistently inclusive trades credibility and possibly success for consensus. If her style is consistently Commanding, she may trade loyalty for obedience. Women who succeed in male-dominated organizations know that cramming your preferred style down the throats of others doesn't work. Becoming one of the boys doesn't work either. The key is to learn how to respond to the demands of the situation at hand by using styles outside your comfort zone. Practice is the best teacher.

The LSI provides a framework for discussing the stereotypes and accompanying dysfunctional communication patterns that block the paths of women seeking senior positions in traditional organizations. For the woman whose preferred style of leadership is supplementary to that of her organization, the road is smoother than it is for the woman who, for example, tends to prefer a Supportive style but works in a company or division where Commanding leadership is expected. Nancy Johnson, a Xerox engineer, had exactly this type of experience. "Command-and-control is the style used most often on the East Coast," she told me. "So when I go there I use that kind of style. When I come back to California, my style changes back to a more supportive, logical one. If I could only communicate in one way I probably couldn't do my job."

As women stretch their styles to meet expectations or the demands of their tasks, disadvantageous stereotypes often complicate the endeavor. Sure, men must face stereotypes too, but that is another book. Women, by virtue of their newness to organizations and limited presence in leadership positions, are "being watched." Having developed a limited range of categories for women's behaviors, men find it easy to move women from one category to another — for example, from "pushover" to "ice queen" — in rather quick succession. While I have not found research support for the observation, my own experiences suggest a tendency for men to label the woman rather than her behavior. This occurred recently when a colleague of mine stopped by the office to discuss my decision to take an unpopular stand on an issue.

Mark: Are you really going to go to bat on that issue?
Me: Yes. I thought you agreed with me.
Mark: I do. But you were the sacrificial lamb last year. Why be it again?

From my perspective, I was merely taking a stand on an issue that made complete sense to me. There was no sacrifice in it. It was the right thing to do. From his perspective I was sacrificing myself for the good of those who follow me. He might have said, "You did your share to help us out last year," but instead he introduced a label that was neither correct nor complimentary. My reply was intended to clarify my actions to him.

Me: Let's back up a bit here. What I did last year was not a sacrifice and, as you know, I'm no lamb. I believed it was the right position to take, so I took it. And it worked for the most part. Others may benefit. I certainly hope so, but what I did was for me, too.

My tone of voice was not defensive or angry. He had just said what was on his mind. I could leave it on his mind or provide a more accurate appraisal of my actions. His response was thoughtful and nondefensive as well. "You're right," he said. "That was the wrong description." I added, "Let's look at it this way: Would you have done the same?" He replied, "Yes, I would have." I probed further. "And would you have been a sacrificial lamb?" "I hope not," he said, smiling.

This interaction could occur between two men or two women. In isolation it isn't terribly problematic. But if women accept the mislabeling of their intentions, actions, and personalities, they contribute to the "stickiness" of disadvantageous stereotypes. When men take up a cause, they are far less likely to be referred to as sacrificial lambs than women. They might be considered "no pushover," "a guy who gives back what he gets," or "a bull in a china shop," but certainly not a lamb.

Research indicates that there exists a host of easy labels for women's actions that contribute to stereotypes. These labels leak into language. As I tell students in my Negotiation and Persuasion classes, when words are used to undermine your goals, revising them on the spot is important.

Dismantling limiting stereotypes requires a refusal to accept them when they are manifest in conversation. Borrowing from President Bush's "Thousand Points of Light," what women need is a thousand little daggers piercing the inflated blimps of devaluing stereotypes.

As I said earlier, your reaction may range from demure to aggressive. The key is to speak up at the time or shortly thereafter. This is the philosophy of an ARCO executive who offered the following comment at a meeting of female leaders held at USC: "I've learned to speak up, something I didn't do twenty years ago. The expectations men have for women are narrow and limiting. I stayed within them for a long time. I gave that up. I've discovered my own potency, my ability to say what I mean and have it heard. You have to be seen to be heard, but you have to be heard to be seen. I used to avoid both for fear of derogatory labels. Not any more; and I've never been happier or more convinced of my own competence."

The capacity to escape the oppression of labels is a prerequisite to female leadership. Throwing off the shackles of stereotypes and the dysfunctional pattern of communication they breed is the first step in clearing the path to leadership for women. It requires recognizing a disadvantageous stereotype and nipping it in the bud. The nipping demands an ability to use language to convince others that the stereotypes no longer apply. Two disadvantageous stereotypes, female emotionality and lowered credibility, are cases in point.

TOO EMOTIONAL TO LEAD?

That women are perceived to be emotional is the first in a series of disadvantageous stereotypes. According to common wisdom, women are more emotional than men. From the book *Women and Sex Roles* comes this description:

Novels, movies, advertisements — all abound with the stereotype that women are more emotional than men. The emotional woman is believed to become flustered in the most minor crisis. She is seen as sensitive, often fearful and anxious, and cries easily. She is moody — sometimes bubbling over with joy; sometimes irritable, lethargic, and depressed.[9]

Research on the emotionality of women is inconsistent. Usually paper-and-pencil tests are used to assess emotional reactions. Given cultural expectations that a "real man" is not fearful or overtly emotional, researchers aren't sure whether men are even willing to write on paper the range of emotions they truly feel. Researchers have attempted to bypass written reports of emotionality by using heartbeat, pulse, respiration and other physiological measures, but those results have been inconsistent as well.[10]

At the very least, women are assumed to be more emotionally expressive than men. This, in organizational environments where emotional suppression is required, can be sufficient reason to block female promotions to senior positions. During a session on conflict for telecommunication managers that I was conducting, one male manager explained: "I hate to say it, but even the possibility of a woman crying in my office is unsettling. Recently I came up with a way to handle it. I keep tissues on my desk. If a woman cries, I hand her the tissues and tell her I'll be back when she is feeling more composed. It gets me out of there so I don't have to deal with it."

This manager may be responding to a personal discomfort with female expression of emotion, but he is also probably influenced by unstated organizational rules. Researchers have proposed that organizational rules requiring the suppression of emotion have as their true purpose the elimination of employee expression. As communication researchers Dennis Mumby and Linda Putnam describe, the supposed rationality of organizations "co-opts emotions" and gives cognition the primary credit for bringing about organizational goals. For men to appear more concerned with the task goals of the organization, they must suppress overt expressions of emotion.[11]

Mumby and Putnam propose that both women and men, though more so women, experience emotional alienation in the course of daily work. Companies employ what organizational expert Arlie Russell

Hochschild describes as the "managed heart" approach to work, which requires employees to suppress anger and exhibit niceness.[12] What's overlooked in this process is the amount of "emotional labor" that employees must put forth to get through each day. Management actually separates people from their natural emotions by requiring that they respond only in ways that are deemed to be appropriate or professional.

If people were primarily cognitive rather than emotional beings, the "managed heart" style of management might meet with greater success. But people are not more cognitive than emotional. And suppression of such a large part of their experience of the world is a trying activity. This may be especially true of women, for whom worksite emotional suppression also means converting any displays of emotion into ones acceptable to men. As with the elevation of hierarchical forms of leadership over network forms, the elevation of rationality over emotion creates for women considerable antagonism between what they've learned are acceptable female displays of emotion and professional requirements.

One example is the misfit between the female tendency to examine issues even if it might strain the relationship and the male preference to work around such issues.[13]

A professor shared with me a story he described as indicative of how men differ from most women. At a faculty meeting, an accounting professor openly disagreed with a finance professor colleague's proposal. Several days later, the disagreeing accounting professor passed by the finance professor in the hall. The accounting professor greeted the finance professor, who responded, "I don't talk to assholes." After that, neither man spoke to the other for months until one day, they passed each other again. This time it was the finance professor who waved and nodded. The accounting professor responded, "I don't talk to assholes" and kept walking. The finance professor caught up with the accounting professor and said, "I don't blame you for that. I was out of line." Since then their relationship has been amicable. They may never be great friends, but they can work with each other comfortably.

The professor related this story to make the point that "somewhere along the way" men learn to put offenses behind them in order to work with each other. Women too are capable of putting emotional rifts behind them and even creating the appearance of doing so, but often they've not been socialized to do so. They prefer to talk through problems, to get to the heart of them. They seek verbal assurance that the same problem will not recur. All this is likely due to the emphasis women place on relational harmony and the common female expectation that friendship involves sharing feelings and talking about interpersonal matters. For men, friendship and co-worker relationships involve doing things together, focusing on activities. Women are used to including in their talk a wide range of topics, whereas men typically restrict their conversations to task and activity talk rather than probing each other's personal thoughts and justifications for behavior.[14]

All of this makes it very difficult for men and women to understand each other, but it also gives women a considerable disadvantage in achieving leadership. Emotional talk is not perceived as masculine, and nonmasculine behaviors are typically considered below leadership quality. The remedy many women have selected is suppression of emotion — hiding their true feelings.

The trouble is that this is not working. Like many actions women have taken to prove themselves worthy of leadership, hiding or suppressing emotion has proven difficult and minimally productive. Managing the heart is exhausting, especially when one's early socialization was contrary to current expectations. The body is not always cooperative in hiding true feelings. Emotional leakage in the course of suppression may be worse than having clearly expressed one's anger or frustration. Negative feelings toward others follow the suppression of emotion, so that one way or the other emotion finds its way into work relationships. In many cases, it's better to guide its arrival rather than allow it to leak endlessly through facial expression, rigid body posture, indirect eye contact, and a host of other bodily responses to negative emotional states. An additional downside of suppressed emotion is that others cannot correct their behavior and so are likely to repeat offenses.

So long as leadership is associated with conviction and confidence, rationality and decisiveness, women will need to decide whether they can afford to express emotion in traditionally female ways or suppress their emotions entirely. The former is risky, and there is much to be said for expanding one's emotional repertoire to include traditionally feminine and masculine ways of emoting. The latter robs people of their passion. It takes away the feeling part of living and relegates the suppressor to neutralness and invisibility. No one can be a neutral leader. Why not experiment? Step outside the boundaries of the expected, risk the labels, and discover, as so many women do, that survival is possible. Sometimes this means making quite clear that you're angry. Women who take this risk often find that the world does not end, they are not fired on the spot, and in fact they garner greater respect. "Female leader" is not nearly the oxymoron that "emotionless leader" is. Until women step outside the narrow range of expected female emotion to experiment, fail, and succeed, they will not become leaders because too much of their own potency will be tied up in emotional labor intended to satisfy men, accomplishing little other than dissatisfying themselves and wasting valuable energy.

LOWERED CREDIBILITY

Credibility is a necessary component of leadership. A host of stereotypes conspire to diminish the capacity of women to achieve credibility in predominantly male environments. I remember well the comment of a male program director who had invited me to speak to telecommunications managers for the third time: "We are always glad we invited you. You're great. After a few minutes the people in the room forget you're a woman."

You've read enough of this book to know that I didn't let it pass. I didn't have to say anything, my face said it all. I looked directly at him and shook my head in disbelief. He knew immediately that his comment had not been received as the compliment he had intended it to be. He assured me that he had meant it as a compliment. He added, "Besides, you know what I meant." I did know what he meant. And he is a genuinely pleasant person. But his words confirmed the inherent credibility liability women bring to most business situations. It was a verbal reflection of an attitude that feeds the stereotype of women as ineffective leaders. Letting his comment pass without some indication that it was not the best way to offer a compliment would have added to the problem.

Communication research has identified five major components of credibility: expertise, conviction, energy, composure, and trust.

Expertise

Expertise is a fundamental component of leadership as well as credibility. For women, this poses a problem, since they are perceived as having less knowledge than men. The value placed on women's expertise is illustrated by what happens when a large number of women enter an occupation: its prestige declines. In most cultures, men's work positions have higher status than those of women. This bias exists despite considerable research evidence that the leadership ability of women does not differ from that of men. Unfortunately for women, their behaviors are evaluated differently. The same style displayed by male and female managers is typically evaluated with a bias favoring men.

Aside from the differential evaluations applied to male and female behavior, attributions for success and failure are also biased. A man's success is more likely to be attributed to ability, a woman's success to hard work, good luck, or an easy task. A woman's failure will be attributed to lack of ability, a man's failure to bad luck, a hard task, or lack of effort.[15]

Nearly every woman I've met in business and academe has experienced devaluation of her abilities. Often it comes in the form of watching male colleagues receive praise for the same behaviors overlooked or berated in women. As I explain to my negotiation students, a single action can be described in either complimentary or derogatory ways. For example, the same behaviors that one person might label "stubborn" can be described more favorably as "persistent," "determined," "a man of conviction." One person's "overachiever" is another's "genius." The man who is "confident" displays the same behaviors as the woman who is "pushy."

Communication experts have a phrase that captures this: "Meanings are in people, not in words." Words themselves are merely vehicles of what people think. Men who believe that women are less competent tend to use words to describe women that diminish the value of what they do even if it is identical to what an admired man does.

Once again, the only way to counteract this tendency to devalue women's work is for women and men to attend to language leaks, clues that devaluation is occurring. For example:

Jim: I hear your report was a hit upstairs.

Marilyn: They seem to like it.

Jim: They were probably pretty impressed with the fact you are a woman too.

Marilyn: What do you mean?

Jim: Nothing. I just meant that they've been really pushing the diversity stuff on us lately, so they must have been delighted to be able to give the project to a woman.

This is not an uncommon conversation. Marilyn has some choices here. Jim has implied that it is the company's diversity program that gave her an advantage rather than her own competence. She could let it pass, assume that he meant nothing, or she could bring this DCP to a timely demise. She might say, "Well, they've been giving it to men this long, it must be a nice break. But if you're suggesting that is why they liked the report, I suggest you read it." This response gets directly at the implication Jim has conveyed. In all likelihood he would respond, "That's not what I meant at all." If so, Marilyn might say, "Funny, it sounded that way to me. But I'll accept your version this time."

Another option is for Marilyn to avoid directly responding to Jim's taunting comments. She could ask: "Have you read my report?" If he says no, her reply is: "Then I guess you can't really judge at this point whether it was gender or superb work that tipped the balance." Then there is the label-swapping approach: "Sounds like sour grapes to me, Jim." Here his labeling her success as the result of "diversity stuff" gives her ample justification for attributing his response to jealousy.

For the woman who detests direct responses to veiled insults, there is always the option to say, "This sounds like a conversation I'd rather not have" or "No offense taken, Jim," which informs him that you didn't miss his intention to devalue your work while not directly insulting him. There are, of course, the lighthearted but clear responses: "I see the green-eyed monster has its grip on you, my friend" or "Thank you so much, Jim, for your obvious support."

No doubt some people cringe to think of themselves responding in any of these ways. Why not let it pass? women have asked me. The answer: Go ahead. Let it pass. But what goes around comes around again, and letting these kinds of comments go unheeded invites their return. All of us live in a symbolic world. Language is used to categorize. If a category is inaccurate, derogatory, or uncomfortable, it must be shed early and/or emphatically or it will stick.

Conviction and Energy

A second dimension of credibility is conviction: the confidence and forcefulness with which something is said or done. When people demonstrate low energy, when there is no passion in their voice, persuasiveness is diminished. Women often have a disadvantage here. The speech patterns of men and women differ in word choice, intonation, volume, and directness. Women use more intensifiers ("most," "better"), modals ("can," "would"), tag questions ("don't you," "didn't you") and requests in question form ("will you please close the door" instead of "close the door") than do men. These suggest uncertainty and a lack of power.[16]

Women frequently use disclaimers before making potentially controversial statements: "I don't want you to take this the wrong way, but . . ." or "I'm not suggesting that anyone is to blame, but . . ." Essentially women apologize for their thoughts. They attempt to avoid relational offense. These kinds of statements, if overused, reduce the conviction of women's speech and thereby threaten their credibility in traditional male-dominated organizations.

A simple answer would be for women to conform their speech to that of men. They could get rid of disclaimers, tag questions, intensifiers, and other patterns more prevalent in female speech. But that is not the solution. It once again places women in the position of becoming other than who and what they are. Rather, women should think about style. Consider whether the current situation calls for direct or indirect speech. It is not necessary that women always speak like the men around them but rather that they can do so when it counts.

Sometimes this means getting to the point more quickly, raising one's voice to be heard, learning phrases that capture attention, employing humor, dropping some disclaimers, and/or being sure you are saying what you mean. For example, if you really need a project completed by 5 P.M., you don't ask a subordinate, "Can you find a way to finish that by 5 P.M.?" You say, "I need that by 5 P.M." Being supportive is a necessary part of leadership, but people need to know when you really need something and when you can wait. The same is true if you have an important point to make at a meeting. Don't embellish it and continually apologize for any possible offense. Say what you mean and see how they take it. If it doesn't work, lighten up a little next time. Trial and error is the only way to expand style.

It wouldn't hurt to try some variation in body language as well. Expressing conviction often requires cooperation of the body — standing up, taking up a larger space, gesturing. All these add energy to conviction. The two can be very persuasive.

Composure

The fourth dimension of credibility is the degree to which an individual appears relaxed, confident, poised. Here again, women have some tendencies that can prove disadvantageous. For example, research has revealed that men are more likely than women to expect to achieve, to judge their own performance more favorably, and to predict that their future performance will be at least as good and possibly better.[17]

Add to this the aforementioned tendency for women to attribute their success to hard work or luck rather than ability and it should come as no surprise that many women are visibly tense in leadership situations. Self-doubt is a powerful enemy of leadership because people expect leaders to be composed and confident.

Most successful women have engaged in considerable composure work. They have taught themselves to trust their judgment, to accept compliments without denying their validity, and to allow themselves the slack occasionally to do less well than they'd hoped. The most effective means of developing composure is frequently observing oneself succeed. It also helps to look around at the body postures of others as they speak. In all likelihood they are somewhat nervous, too. Taking courses in public speaking can be useful. Most important, women need to recognize that their socialization has encouraged self-doubt in the majority of cases. This means that they are willing receptacles of criticism. There is nothing wrong with constructive criticism, but taking it to heart and using it to reinforce feelings of insecurity is another means by which women usher themselves out of the line to leadership. There is nothing wrong with occasional nervousness or self-doubt; but it's wrong to let other people use it to make you wonder whether you can lead.

Trust

The final criterion of credibility that can prove a roadblock for women is the human tendency to trust people like ourselves. Women and minorities are different from the majority of workers in traditional organizations. This alone is often sufficient reason for distrust. In order to make the world a more predictable, orderly, less threatening place, people categorize others. People who share such things as the same religion, birthplace, sports interests, number of children, or color preference can find through conversation that they have something in common. This commonality may be rather insignificant, but it serves as a foundation of understanding for the discovery of other commonalities.

For women in primarily male work environments, their differences are more obvious than their similarities to the people in power, the people who select leaders. Here again, there's an opportunity to overturn stereotypes of women as different from men and less capable by finding commonalities and using them to minimize differences. This means finding opportunities in conversation to discuss what you have in common with male co-workers rather than assuming that the differences between you are too great.

One female business consultant did this by learning about sports. Whenever I was with her I'd marvel at her ability to talk about baseball, basketball, football, and soccer. She knew the teams and the players. She could talk about the coaches' faults and even slipped into sports jargon when talking with male business executives or taxi drivers.

It isn't necessary to learn sports if it isn't a frequent part of conversation at work, but it's important to find out what interests the people with whom you work. Reading up a bit on mountain biking isn't a bad idea if your boss is an avid fan. Taking a few golf lessons is useful in some organizations. Sometimes all that's needed is a willingness to learn enough to ask good questions.

This applies to men as well. I recently witnessed a conversation between a female director and a male subordinate. They were talking about her doll collection. He related to her interest in dolls by describing the efforts he and his relatives had expended in their search for the perfect collection doll for his wife. This young man made a positive impression. He didn't have to become a doll collector to relate to his boss's interest. Similarly, women don't have to become football or baseball enthusiasts to relate to a male boss who is one. Learning about the teams and their records is often enough to carry on a conversation.

LOOKING THE LEADER

The task of overcoming stereotypes regarding female credibility would be demanding enough if it depended only on the verbal expressions of women. But it does not. Both women and men hold women to some very high standards in terms of dress.

Deborah Tannen described a double standard of business attire in her June 20, 1993, *New York Times* piece. Tannen noted at a meeting that the four women seated around the table were all dressed differently while the eight men looked much the same. As she considered the variety of clothes the women had worn during the three-day conference, she suddenly wondered why she hadn't been scrutinizing the men's styles as well. Tannen's conclusion: "The men's styles were unmarked." Tannen explained, "The term 'marked' is a staple of linguistic theory. It refers to the way language alters the base meaning of a word by adding a linguistic particle that has no meaning on its own. The unmarked form of a word carries the meaning that goes without saying — what you think of when you're not thinking anything special."[18]

In the case of the male and female conference attendees, the men were unmarked; that is, nothing about them added much information beyond the basic fact that they were male. Each of the women had made decisions regarding hair, clothing, and accessories. Each carried meaning. Tannen explained, "Each of those styles available to us was marked. The men in our group had made decisions too, but the range from which they chose was incomparably narrower. Men can choose styles that are marked, but they don't have to, and in this group none did. Unlike the women, they had the option of being unmarked."[19]

Men do not always have the option to remain unmarked in business settings. At higher levels of traditional organizations, the wrong kind of watch, poor taste in suits or ties, or wearing the wrong type of clothes or shoes to a golf game can spell disaster in terms of being considered "leadership material."

For women in traditional organizations, though, marking opportunities begin early. The hair, clothing, and accessory choices women make contribute to their image. There is no single cross-organization standard female style of dress. There is no single look, although there is a range of looks that are more professional than others. I am very aware of this as a business consultant. What I wear as a professor is important, but less so than what I wear when I speak in public, attend business meetings, or provide consultation. There is one almost "standard" aspect of female senior managers: they tend to have manicured hands. I've rarely stepped into an office where the women's nails are not perfect. One exception is Patagonia. They make clothing for outdoor camping, mountain climbing, and sports. On my first visit to their offices I was decidedly overdressed. It was one of the few days that my nails were appropriately polished for consultation, but there were few manicured nails among the women I met. In fact, there were few dresses. A "marked woman" at Patagonia is one who does have her nails done, her hair perfectly coiffed, and who wears a designer dress with matching shoes.

The Patagonias of the world aside, there is a business look for women. It's usually expensive. It may be the reason why women talk about each other's clothes so much. The other day, I joined an ongoing conversation among four other women. They were discussing a dress worn by an assistant professor. She said, "This is a designer dress. Guess how much I paid for it." We all guessed in the $150 range. "No," she said with deserved delight. "I paid fifteen dollars for it at T. J. Maxx." We all promptly memorized the name and directions to this dress-for-less Mecca and proceeded on our way. I can say for a fact that I have never heard my male colleagues go on about their suits, ties, or shoes. It isn't an issue. They aren't "marked" every day by their choices, not unless they choose to be by wearing a unique tie.

If women are obsessed with clothing, it is because they know it speaks to others. Their choices are meaningful. Like it or not, a manicure says, "This mother of two and senior vice president is so together that she finds time to polish her nails." Not long ago, a rushed morning with the children prevented me from transferring my wallet, pens, and other paraphernalia from a casual carrier to a more sophisticated pocketbook. It did not pass unnoticed at a meeting several hours later. A woman said to me, pointing at my casual bag, "Is this yours?" I replied, "Yes. Thank you for getting it for me." She chuckled in apparent disbelief, "You're kidding. This is really yours?" "Why yes it is," I replied, trying to appear nonplussed. "It just doesn't look like it should be," she added. We dropped the conversation there. I knew what she meant. My style was more sophisticated than this casual carrier conveyed. It marked me as not so altogether together as she thought I was. The next time I saw her I was back to being together — everything matched and was consistent with some unstated image of competence and composure achieved, I might add, in the midst of chaos.

Clothes are not the only aspects of women's work behavior that mark them. In companies where women are few and far between at senior levels, nearly everything women do is marked. Women stand out. So most choose to stand out in style — to look the part, so to speak. Lots of silk, pure fabrics, expensive shoes, and serious jewelry keep women from being marked in a negative way. The woman who does not dress the role, whose hair has no style and nails have no color, may be perceived as not having what it takes to be a professional or a leader.

This was taken to somewhat of an extreme early in Pepsi's history. At one time, Pepsi hired only people who had the "Pepsi look." They came to be called the "Pepsi Pretty." Although one Pepsi senior manager told me that the term was originally used to refer to men as well as women, he explained that it came to be associated more with women. It referred to good-looking, well-groomed, appropriately dressed female Pepsi employees. Times have changed at Pepsi. Several of their people have told me, "We aren't so 'pretty' anymore." They come in all shapes, sizes, and backgrounds. But likely there is still a remnant or two of past expectations that impinge on current practice. This remnant of past influence exists in most companies, so it pays to do some historical research to learn what you're up against.

A West Coast female senior vice president limits the possibility of being "marked" merely because she is female. "All my clothes are selected by a consultant who knows my work style. I wear fashionable but conservative suits every day. There is variation in color and in the blouse, but nothing dramatic. I look professional, not dowdy. People compliment me on my suits, mostly because they are of good quality. Essentially I do the same as the men at my level. They also wear fashionable but conservative suits. They vary their ties, but you can count on them looking pretty much the same each day. That's how I dress too. It works for me just as it works for them."

Many women don't care to be limited to suits. They choose fashionable dresses made of quality materials. When meeting with clients, they may wear a jacket over the dress. The need for this attention to the leadership look depends on the organization and your level in it. You don't want to outdress the boss. The main thing is that being a leader means looking the part whether you are female or male. If that means designer jeans in your company, then it's wise to have some on hand for important meetings. In most companies jeans are out, except on "dress down days" when people are allowed to wear what they please. On other days, leadership calls for setting the tone in all that you do. Dress, unfortunately for the wallet, is no exception. So it's wise to get some professional assistance if looking the leader doesn't come naturally. From head to toe, hair to feet, women are gauged for promotions. If you're going to be "marked," it may as well be for your class, sophistication, eye for quality, and self-regard. These are the markings of a female leader in most organizations.

Just Call Me Doctor

On the topic of high self-regard as it applies to credibility, let me take a moment to point out a disparity in practice that gets in the way of women's progress. I recently met with a group of nurse managers who are working with doctors to revise the culture of their organization. They described how the doctors rely on them as colleagues and that as a teaching facility they are ahead of most medical organizations in their leveling of the playing field between doctors and nurse managers. For example, the director of internal medicine nursing explained that going to a case management orientation has given nurses more power. They can now override doctors when deciding the ward where a patient should be placed.

They were quite pleased with the new recognition that they too can make good decisions. And they had certainly made progress in convincing doctors that care of patients is a team endeavor. But I followed this discussion with a question: "How do the doctors address you?" I asked. The three women smiled at each other. They had apparently discussed the topic before. The nurse manager for surgery said, "We call them by their first names and they do the same with us." I had not expected that answer. It was good to see that, at least in this medical facility, respect could be accorded equally. I probed further. "What do the patients call you?" I asked. She replied with some hesitancy, knowing full well where I was going with my question, "Well, they call the doctors Doctor and us by our first names." We talked for a few minutes about this. One of the nurse managers mentioned that the common thinking on this is that patients feel more comfortable with someone they can call by their first name. But is this an assumption or is it fact? Wouldn't patients prefer to be surrounded by professionals who can make life-and-death decisions. If nurses are now receiving advanced degrees and making significant decisions about patient care, shouldn't they, like doctors, be respected for their professionalism? Shouldn't the doctor address them as Nurse Smith or Nursing Director Jones? Even Mrs. Smith is better than Vicki or Kathy.

One of the nurse managers agreed. "It's more important to me that patients respect the nurses' credentials and opinions so that when we request something of them, they don't consider us unqualified. It's hard to deliver good care if the patient thinks you're just baby-sitting."

"There are some specialties," Connie Noblet, R.N. and founder of the National Organization for Victims Assistance, told me, "where first names help. Rape victims, for example, may benefit from being able to address by first name the people helping them. But it's also true that a first-name basis for nurses can be counterproductive. In most cases it diminishes their credibility with patients and doctors."

She added, "First names may meet the needs of the caregivers more than the patients. You can either feed your own ego or do the job. It's nice to be liked, but exercising your professional skills is more important. Sometimes you can do both. I tell you, though, I'm not sure where the idea came from that nurses should bond with patients and doctors shouldn't, but it's wrong. Specialties like pediatrics might favor first names for good reasons. If so, then the doctors should be, for example, Doctor Bob and the nurses, Nurse Jean. The importance of bonding as compared to professional distance must be weighed for both doctors *and* nurses."

For those who believe this is not relevant and that referring to doctors as Doctor and nurses by their first name is no indication of status, a female ultrasound expert suggests the following test: "If the doctors insist on knowing the first names of the doctors to whom they return phone calls, then you know there's a status game going on."

For those who think titles are a distasteful way of raising oneself over others, it's wise also to remember that in many organizations they determine who talks to whom. One public relations professional told me: "My CEO combs through the names and titles on a conference roster before deciding whether to attend. He wants to be sure he is with people at his level or above."

It's true that titles can be empty, meaningless forms of self-promotion. A person who does not have the experience and competence to back up a title is in for trouble. There is nothing wrong with using first names, at least not in the United States. But it's important to determine whether your desire to be friendly and casual is impeding your ability to be accorded the same respect as male peers. If they are referred to as Doctor or introduced as Vice President, Senior Director, or Distinguished Professor, then use your title too. You worked for it.

GETTING A TRACK RECORD — GETTING CREDIT

There is an unwritten hard-and-fast rule in business that most people learn early in their careers: Make your boss look good. The only trouble with this rule is the tendency of many bosses not to reciprocate. One of my Executive MBA students worked for over a year on a project for his company. It was a creative idea destined to be noticed if handled correctly. He provided his boss with progress reports. When it was time to introduce it to the higher-ups, guess who was left out of the loop? The project and credit were usurped. This thirty-five-year-old student's reaction: "That's the name of the game. But knowing so doesn't keep it from burning in my gut. He could at least have mentioned my name."

American business has been hierarchical for decades. With the advent of team mentalities, some of the credit-snatching is abating. But it has not disappeared from the landscape. People with political savvy know it's important to help the boss look good. They also know, though, that not all bosses can be relied upon to return the favor. In such cases, it is important to make other allies. Bosses come and go. If you dedicate yourself to someone who leaves before providing you some assistance, considerable time has been lost.

"I never put all my apples in one basket," a female vice president explains. "I find reasons to help people. Don't get me wrong. I help my boss too. But he isn't the only person who will determine my future, so I spread the wealth." This is especially important in traditional organizations with few women at the top. When it comes time for promotion, the guys at the top will ask each other, "Has she distinguished herself in any way? What contributions has she made? Is she a team player? Can she take the heat?" and a host of other questions. They may not be worded exactly this way, but they'll be there nonetheless. If a woman has not stood out but rather spent all her time making someone else look good, she may contribute to her own professional demise.

Women are often hesitant to let people know they've canceled a vacation to attend a meeting. They think it is just expected. Not at all. If people don't know you had other plans but canceled them to help them out, they can't credit you. If you watch how men do this, you come to realize that leveraging is an art — a communication art — and one at which most women are not yet terribly proficient.

Women need to think of themselves as having talents the organization needs. It isn't enough to have and offer them, though. Getting credit is key here. Women, even at senior levels, often serve on too many committees. They fail to say, "No, thank you." But worse, they believe serving is sufficient to demonstrate value. Nothing could be further from the truth. If you are going to exert energy, it ought to be for something, not just to be a good citizen or to pay the appropriate dues.

A considerable difference exists between working hard and working smart. As mentioned in Chapter 2, Anne Huff has written that women become "organizational wives" at work. They handle details, remember people's birthdays, spend hours listening to people and getting nothing from it, and serve as good "cheerleaders."[20] Women allow people to make exorbitant claims on their time. Men seem to expect it, so women tend to provide it. Here again the 75 Percent Rule applies: If you are willing to sacrifice yourself for everyone else's benefit, you contribute to the slowing or demise of your own career.

A thirty-two-year-old attorney had the experience of spending several hours on the phone with a man who told her, "I'm not satisfied with my attorney. I trust your judgment over his." She took this to mean that he intended to change attorneys. After several hours of providing valuable information at no cost, she finally asked him, "Am I your attorney or not?" He told her he'd have to think about it and get back to her. The next day he called. "I can't switch attorneys," he said. "Don't get me wrong. You're a far better attorney. But in this case I need a gruff guy like him defending me."

She was appalled. "What nerve," she told me. "He wasted my time and then went with the other attorney because he needed a man to defend him. He didn't exactly say that, but that is what he meant." She gave away her expertise at no cost. This happens to men, but more often to women. Many men expect to pay less for advice from women.

Men are more likely to make it clear when they've gone out of their way. They value their time and can make it darn hard for someone else to place demands on it. If they do, they'd better be grateful. Women haven't mastered this. Most prefer to be seen as helpful. It's admirable, really, but as Benjamin Franklin advised, "Everything in moderation." Being helpful is wonderful. It should be everyone's business. Taking everyone else's monkey on your back, though, makes you a packhorse — and a tired one. It's important to have a red flag alert go off in your brain when someone wants you to do something for nothing. *Here comes one of those "get nothing" requests* is what you should hear in your brain. The next thing you should hear is your mouth saying, "Wish I could help, but I'm scheduled for weeks on other projects."

I have to admit that you are getting this advice from someone for whom being helpful has always seemed a preferable way to live. But I've learned to differentiate between those who deserve help and those who don't. My male colleagues deserve the credit here, some for sharing with me strategies for doing what pays off and some for teaching me by example. I've learned how to handle the "bull in the china shop" who places demands on me and expects me to carry them out without a word of protest or compromise. I go work with someone else. I've learned to deal with the guy who always sends needy, long-winded people to me. I send needy, long-winded people to him, too. And I've learned to respond to people who insist that only I can do some ridiculously simple but time-consuming task. I suggest we share it. If he refuses, I refuse too.

Then there are the people who ask you to do things because only you can do it well. This is flattering, but is often untrue. Other people may not do it as well, or other people may do it well but be unwilling to do it for as little as you're being paid, but there is usually someone who can fill your shoes. If you feel you must give in to such requests, it is unwise to do so without negotiating some benefits that allow you to meet your own goals as well. You should hear yourself saying, "I'll do it under the following conditions." This should be followed by a well-thought-out list of what you need to meet your own goals if you intend to try to meet someone else's at the same time. It may be more secretarial assistance, additional pay, travel related to the project or to one that you must postpone to do the requested project, a change in the due date, and/or better computer equipment. If you are going to help someone meet his needs, he should be willing to help you meet yours. Occasionally this means refusing to listen to flattery, attempts to make you feel guilty, or suggestions that you've become callous. Remind him that it isn't anything personal, just a matter of common sense. Stick to the main claim, which is if you're going to do what he wants, you'll need some things too.

These responses reflect the four major leadership styles.

THE COMMANDING: "I'll do X, but only if you do Y."

THE LOGICAL: "If I'm going to do X, I'll have to postpone projects A and B. So it follows that I'll need to have Y."

THE INSPIRATIONAL: "We're both hoping to reach goals that require the other. To accommodate my vision and yours, both of us may have to stretch ourselves. In my case it means doing X. In yours, doing Y."

THE SUPPORTIVE: "There is nothing I'd like more than to help you on this. You're a friend and a colleague. But I can't see how I'll be able to do it without Y."

Whatever your preferred style, the outcome should be that you are doing work that will help you meet your goals. The goals may occasionally be vague, and a certain amount of helping others who cannot yet help you is important. But when someone is clearly in the position to reciprocate and refuses to do so, it's often wise to help someone else.

No one can be all places at once. Those who try often wear out. The key is to be selective and to ensure that most of what you do leads, as Peter Drucker suggests in *The Effective Executive,* to important goals.[21] Sometimes this means helping someone just because he needs and deserves help. That's fine. In all cases, though, selectivity is crucial. It means using your brain not your heart when saying, "Okay, I'll do it."

‖ 6 ‖

POWER PLAYS AND DISPLAYS

AT THE HEART of leadership is power — a fact of life in business. Those who have it are influential. Power is an aspect of social reality that many have tried desperately to remove from organizations. Making companies smaller, less hierarchical, or more democratic does not rid them of power, it merely changes the way it is used, played, and displayed. No amount of talk about empowering employees can completely erase the existence of power structures. For women to succeed in traditional organizations they must make it their business to understand how power is garnered and used in their companies — both overtly and covertly.

This chapter is all about power plays and displays — how power is used to maintain status and the ways it is demonstrated in the process of achieving objectives. As with leadership, you'll find that some of the uses of power in this chapter fit your style and some of them don't. It pays to be aware of them in any case. Power is largely a matter of perception — who has the resources, who can get the job done, who can be trusted, who has the title, who has the know-how, and who's in the know. There is a difference between holding a position of power and having power. Often people have titles but lack decision-making authority. Some have authority but cannot access necessary resources. Others have titles and authority but lack the expertise needed to reach company and personal goals. It behooves anyone who wants to do well in an organization to understand the many forms that power takes. For women this is especially true.

GETTING BEYOND POWER STEREOTYPES

Common wisdom has it that women possess less desire than men for power, but research indicates otherwise. David McClelland, a leading expert in power and motivation and author of *Power: The Inner Experience,* believes that it is not so much power needs as it is expressions of power that distinguish men and women.[1] Some research suggests that women are characteristically interested in internal strength, while men are more interested in power in the service of performing tasks and dealing with environmental demands.[2] These different orientations lead to different expressions of power as well.

Power is defined here as the ability to get people to do things they wouldn't have done otherwise. The powerful person uses reward, coercion, status, similarity, expertise, or information to influence others.[3] Stereotypically, women are supposed to act as though they aren't using such direct forms of power as coercion and status. They are expected to be indirect — even manipulative — rather than direct and commanding.[4]

Early in a woman's career, the inability to use direct power is usually not a deterrent to advancement. This changes, though, as she moves into managerial positions. As mentioned in Chapter 1, the "cute-and-little" stage isn't threatening. Young women can comfortably ask for help and play supportive roles that let them associate with people in power. They may find rewarding use of such indirect forms of influence as being helpful and showing admiration for superiors. At this stage, the positive responses from their male associates may leave them wondering, "What's all the fuss about women getting ahead in business?" But soon thereafter, they learn that women who want to advance to senior levels must obtain and use power, not merely associate with those who have it. Traditional organizational stereotypes keep them from doing so in the same ways men do. Women are supposed to act as though they aren't using power.

Women who accommodate their behaviors to these stereotypes hesitate to admit they desire power. As a result, they fail to learn how to obtain and use power. The power plays and displays men learn are inaccessible to many women who are discouraged from experimenting with such techniques. But there are women who have bypassed stereotypes and made power a tool. One such woman told me why she has been able to garner and exert power: "I was brought up in New York. Where I lived, you had to learn to take care of yourself. But it's more than that. I look like I could be dangerous. My voice, my physique, are scary to a lot of people. They don't want to mess with me."

There's something to be said for looking like you could make other people's lives difficult. A number of women I've met personify Machiavelli's advice that "one ought to be both feared and loved, but as it is difficult for the two to go together, it is much safer to be feared than loved, if one of the two has to be wanting."[5]

Most of the women I've met who convey power are actually quite pleasant, even nurturant once you get to know them, but they've adopted Machiavelli's philosophy that "it is well to seem merciful, faithful, humane, sincere, religious, and also to be so; but you must have the mind so disposed that when it is needful to be otherwise you may be able to change to the opposite qualities."[6]

As with leadership, variability of style in the application of power is key. Machiavelli's advice was often harsh, but there is much to be learned from reading *The Prince*. Consider these styles: The Commanding leader wants absolute power. The Logical leader prefers to use power to achieve reasonable objectives. The Inspirational leader is willing to share power in the pursuit of a common goal. The Supportive leader prefers the power of connections with others to the more common controlling form.

Machiavelli recognized the value of being able to express power in a variety of ways depending on the situational demands. When constrained to only the more pleasant power displays, women find a significant segment of leadership expression inaccessible to them. For those women who don't have a commanding look, who lack a voice and physique that shout, "Watch your step with me," stereotypes and their own physiognomy combine to curtail their access to more direct forms of power expression.

A *Business Week* report entitled "Women Entrepreneurs" echoed the increasingly popular view that the reason why women leave traditional businesses to become entrepreneurs is so they can utilize their natural tendency to be nurturant and supportive. It seems that business has found a new niche for women — the nurturant, supportive, sensitive entrepreneur. This is yet another easy attribution in the long list of popular attempts to categorize women in simple fashion. The reality is that entrepreneurship often requires tough, direct, confident, convincing behavior. When female entrepreneurs treat their people in a humane way, they nonetheless expect and, when need be, demand good work. Many of the women running successful entrepreneurial ventures would have made the traditional companies that lost them more profitable had they been given half a chance. Female business owners who are comfortable with expressions of sensitivity and nurturance are most certainly running their businesses in a nontraditional manner. As business people, however, they know they must make clear what they expect in the way of work and achievement.[7]

THE VARIED EXPRESSIONS OF POWER

With the fiction of the supportive, sensitive woman entrepreneur behind us, the important point about power is that it may take on a variety of forms. Women should observe and determine how to expand beyond their preferred styles to incorporate new power techniques. So equipped, they can flexibly meet the demands of a variety of work situations. This does not mean sacrificing your own preferences. If you enjoy being sensitive, supportive, and encouraging of teamwork, by all means don't stop. But as so many women at the top of traditional companies have found, even when you don't intend to speak like the natives, it's good to know what they're up to.

The Art of War, written by the Chinese philosopher Sun Tzu more than 2,500 years ago, is another book that offers important guidance. Sun Tzu's writing was intended as a text for battlefield victory, yet many executives have found valuable lessons in its pages. Sun Tzu knew that direct tactics alone cannot win a war.

There are not more than five musical notes, yet the combinations of these five give rise to more melodies than can ever be heard. There are not more than five primary colors, yet in combination they produce more hues than can ever be seen. There are not more than five cardinal tastes — sour, acrid, salt, sweet, bitter — yet combinations of them yield more flavors than can ever be tasted. In battle, however, there are not more than two methods of attack — the direct and the indirect; yet these two in combination give rise to an endless series of maneuvers.[8]

So it is with leadership styles and associated preferences for direct and indirect expressions of power. Relying on only one style limits your options and leads to labels — "demure" and "aggressive" among them. Learning how to go beyond personal limits in acquiring and using power is key. Transferable knowledge is more important to a career than firm-specific knowledge, according to Rosabeth Moss Kanter.[9] Thus, if women hesitate to explore power in its various forms, they risk not only being overlooked at their current job but also being unprepared for a job or career change.

My experience as a college debater taught me a valuable lesson: It's not enough to know you are right. You must know how the other side thinks. You must know the reasoning of your opponents as well as you know your own. This lesson applies to business too. If you want to succeed in an environment where others think and act differently from you, understanding them is crucial. In this context, acquiring transferable knowledge means becoming a student of power in its various forms, learning what works for others and for yourself. It means coming to understand how power is acquired and expressed in an effort to expand your own repertoire.

POWER PLAYS

Among the many ways of expressing power are ones that can be characterized as power plays. These behaviors preserve power for those who possess it, but accomplish little else. A desire for power is natural; it helps us exert some control over our own fate. But when it becomes an obsession, a more intense motivation than achieving the objectives for which power was required in the first place, power plays take hold.

John O'Neil, author of *The Paradox of Success,* differentiates between power in the service of worthy accomplishments and power as an end in itself. Often, control becomes the end rather than the means. When power is employed this way, much time is wasted. Take the administrator who delays responding to requests to make others aware of his ability to make their lives difficult. Power-playing bosses assign menial tasks to subordinates just to let them know who's boss or "make people jump" by requiring them to complete demanding tasks in ridiculously short periods of time.[10]

Some power players like to use loyalty tests, enlisting subordinates in their efforts to make life difficult for the people they dislike. Others expect subordinates to arrive at work early because that is when they arrive. Among the loyalty tests described by Pat Heim and Susan Golant in their book *Hardball for Women* is the boss who expected his people to cease doing business with a particular car dealership because he had difficulty with them — another boss expected male subordinates to demonstrate their loyalty by wearing ties manufactured by his wife's company.[11]

Some managers call meetings without warning just to keep people aware of who's boss. Some make frequent, illogical demands. Others expect to dominate conversations. These power plays come from what O'Neil describes as "rampant ego-inflation or hubris." Believing your own public relations is perhaps a more simply descriptive term for what happens when the attainment of power becomes the primary goal.[12]

Women are capable of self-inflation and hubris, but are brought up to be less comfortable with power that alienates. Women learn to judge themselves in terms of their connectedness. For most women, power equates to connections, not fear. A steady diet of autocratic power isolates. In her book *In a Different Voice* Carol Gilligan describes the predominant metaphor of women's lives as a web. For men, it is hierarchy. The two are quite different. As Gilligan writes:

> The images of hierarchy and web, drawn from the texts of men's and women's fantasies and thoughts, convey different ways of structuring relationships and are associated with different views of morality and self. As the top of the hierarchy becomes the edge of the web and as the center of the network of connection becomes

the middle of a hierarchical progression, each image marks as dangerous the place which the other defines as safe. Thus the images of hierarchy and web inform different modes of assertion and response: the wish to be alone at the top and the consequent fear that others will get too close; the wish to be at the center of connection and the consequent fear of being too far out on the edge. These disparate fears of being stranded and being caught give rise to different portrayals of achievement and affiliation, leading to different modes of action and different ways of assessing the consequences of choice.[13]

Gilligan believes that, for women, hierarchy is unstable, lonely, and often morally problematic. Raising children reinforces the need for connectedness. It requires women, who still bear the greatest responsibility in this area, to teach ethics and justice. In so doing, women reinforce these values in themselves. We see the same kind of self-persuasion in men who share or have the responsibility of child rearing.[14]

Values need not be divorced from power, but they are often perceived to be. Power can be helpful, but it is often selfish. Hence the common wisdom: Power corrupts. Henry David Thoreau wrote:

> Rather than love, than money, than fame, give me truth. I sat at a table where were rich food and wine in abundance, and obsequious attendance, but sincerity and truth were not; and I went away hungry from the inhospitable board. The hospitality was as cold as the ices. I thought that there was no need of ice to freeze them. They talked to me of the age of the wine and the fame of the vintage; but I thought of an older, a newer, and purer wine, of a more glorious vintage, which they had not got, and could not buy. The style, the house and grounds and "entertainment" pass for nothing with me. I called on the king, but he made me wait in his hall, and conducted himself like a man incapacitated for hospitality. There was a man in my neighborhood who lived in a hollow tree. His manners were truly regal. I should have done better had I called on him.[15]

Thoreau's desire for true hospitality is similar to the desire women have for connectedness. The abhorrence of shallow shows of greatness is like their distaste for power without compassion for people. Let me be clear: Women are not inherently better than men. But their development makes them less willing to accept power as the ultimate measure of people, especially if that power is what Warren Bennis labels "positional power." In *The Invented Self,* Bennis describes how such power leaves the owner "without influence or voice." When women achieve positional power or in most cases just get near it, many recognize and find unappealing its price of relational disconnection.[16]

POWER DISPLAYS

In *Managing with Power,* Jeffrey Pfeffer writes: "To be successful in getting things done in organizations, it is critical that you be able to diagnose the relative power of the various participants and comprehend the patterns of interdependence."[17] It's also important to learn what is lost and what is gained by engaging in behaviors that communicate power.

Deference

Power often derives its credibility from subordinates' displays of deference, their treating the power holder better than those around him. A good part of what is referred to as "the trappings of power" is the degree of attention and responsiveness provided to people who are considered powerful. Women are capable of deference, but they're not raised to value it as a way of succeeding in life. Highly competent women want to get to the top because they deserve to be there, not because they "kissed up" all along the way.

Attorney General Janet Reno has demonstrated her unwillingness to be obsequious even to the President of the United States. Reno inherited from her grandmother and mother what *Time* magazine describes as a "passionate commitment to duty and family." Even her fiercest critics acknowledge her "ethical hygiene." This same article quotes a White House administration official describing Reno: "It just so happens that she's very, very good and responsible. She's not personally ambitious. I don't think it's particularly important to her that the President like her. If she were power-mad, it would be dangerous."[18]

Among women who reach senior levels without showing excessive deference, who perceive more than one path to success, many encourage subordinates to treat them as team leaders rather than superiors. With companies becoming increasingly team oriented and organizational structures becoming flatter, the capacity to lead in nonautocratic ways can prove useful. But there is a limit. As one successful entrepreneur and self-proclaimed "female power maven" explained to me: "There is a lot to be said for being nurturant and soliciting people's opinions. I see no reason why people in power have to look like the CEO who is the only one not carrying something as he walks down the hall with four other people. But there is one downside to sharing power. When a crisis occurs, you have to be able to make decisions, delegate and get things done. If you can't do that, no one is going to want you running the show."

Another downside is that men accustomed to traditional displays of deference on a daily basis — what the woman quoted above terms a "plantation mentality" — often interpret the power-sharing approach to work as an absence of respect on the part of the female manager's people. When determining whether she should be promoted to a more senior position, they may hesitate in the belief that she won't be able to command respect and give direction when it counts.

This is the trade-off women must face in deciding to lead in supportive, nonautocratic ways. Some people will always interpret it as indecisiveness. These same people will interpret the absence of people deferring to you as the absence of leadership potential. You can change your style to please them, leave it be and hope they recognize the benefits, find another job, or, some time when it counts, let them see that you can be commanding too.

The Power in Style

In Chapter 3 I discussed the effort Xerox has made toward creating an environment where men and women are heard. When interrupted, people at any level of the company may say, "You shut me out." Drawing attention to verbal bullying has helped both women and men at Xerox feel their ideas are more welcome. No doubt, there are times when people fail to live up to the Xerox standard, but the company has seriously endeavored to ensure that people are comfortable speaking up. This culture of openness facilitated Nancy Johnson's ascent to the position of chief engineer, but it was her own competence and flexibility of style that clinched it.

"I watch how my style affects people. I engage in ongoing moderation. You have to have different styles down, up, and sideways," Johnson told me. "I try to work in ways that I'm of most assistance to people, so we do things well together. If the president calls, I'm not going to say, 'What do you think, Paul?' I'll answer in simple, declarative sentences. But if one of my direct reports calls, I might ask what he thinks. We might work it out together. I tend to be supportive-giving with my people as much as possible. With upper levels I'm controlling-taking, and somewhere in between with people at my level."

Before 1985 most Xerox engineers had controlling-taking styles; they told people what to do. They interrupted and talked over incessantly, and Johnson learned how to do that too. In fact, she is still training herself to stop talking over now that people have learned to listen to each other. "As the only woman I had to talk over to be heard. I'm still doing it, but I'm trying to quit."

Johnson learned how to manage her style by watching and listening to others, particularly people with whom she shared little with regard to style. "I learn from everybody; not just the people I like. They are too similar," she says. "One of my bosses was very controlling. He met individually with each of his people one time a week for two hours. I hated that. I never took problems to him. So eventually he cancelled some of the meetings with me. But other people brought him all their problems. They transferred the monkey to his back. I didn't like that. People should solve their own problems to the extent they can do so. So, when my boss moved on and I was promoted to his position, I stopped the meetings. I thought everyone would be relieved. I later learned that my direct reports thought my not meeting with them meant I didn't care. We got together and talked about it. Now they know I care. The change of management caused misunderstanding. Now they bring some problems to me. We work them out, but I don't take the monkey on my back. We share it.

"I've learned that one style doesn't work for everyone," Johnson continues. "In Rochester, New York, the senior managers tend to be controlling-taking. On the West Coast, we're more entrepreneurial. The styles are a hundred and eighty degrees out, but both regions are successful. Consistency and fit are what matter most. You need to tell people what you're doing, then they know what to expect."

Johnson has a useful technique for dealing with people who aren't listening to her. "Sometimes two people will be talking in the back of the room. Rather than ask them to stop," she says, "I'll begin a sentence in a way that makes it sound like the information to follow is very important. For example, I'll say, 'The most incredible thing that is going to happen to Xerox in . . .' Then I'll stop talking. People will all be waiting quietly for me to finish. I'll look at the two people in the back of the room. Wait for them to stop talking — which they will. Then I'll continue."

It's important for women to develop ways to hold the floor. Women's voices are softer. When they use tentative speech patterns over and over, men just tune them out. It isn't always purposely rude; in traditional organizations men aren't inclined to listen to people who introduce ideas in ways that make them sound unimportant. Time is money, as the saying goes. If people qualify everything they say, nothing they say appears to have merit.

I teach my students to select from among their ideas the ones they really want others to hear and remember. The rest is what I call "claim clutter" — ideas that distract you from your purpose and direct the discussion away from productive closure. A male CEO of a major U.S. consumer electronics firm recently shared with me his belief that most people don't know how to reach closure.

According to this CEO, most senior-level people fail to separate out those issues that might be easily resolved from those that need more study. As a result, unnecessary committees are formed, small issues grow into large ones, and a lot of work doesn't get done while people distract themselves with issues that might have been more easily resolved.

Taking a lesson from my conversation with him, the next week I made a concerted effort to apply what I've come to think of as The Closure Rule: Whenever possible resolve rather than complicate. Advise subordinates, "When you arrive at my door with a problem, please bring along one or two solutions as well. Let me know which situations require my attention immediately and let's try to help each other reach closure as effectively and efficiently as possible." It's impossible to function effectively when everything is a crisis. No one can or should be handling every issue that comes along. It doesn't pay to get wrapped up in the emotion of the moment or to allow solvable issues to drag on, sapping everyone's time and energy. Power is lost in wasted time.

Clarity and Brevity

In an average one-hour presentation, people listen attentively for about twenty minutes. The rest of the time they may be thinking about lunch or next Saturday's golf excursion. This poses a real dilemma for a presenter. If every idea is presented with the same level of emphasis, few of those ideas are likely to be remembered. For effectiveness, it's necessary to emphasize the most significant ideas. In any speech — or conversation for that matter — some bits of information are more valuable than others. This presents a choice: You can let people decide what to remember, or you can do some of the work for them. One way is to add phrases and adjectives to describe key points. For example, "If you don't remember anything else I've said today, remember . . ." tells people that what you're about to say is important. Words such as "interesting," "vital," "key," "fundamental," and "instrumental" give weight and power to ideas. Add nonverbal gestures of emphasis, and people are more likely to listen. Without them, people spend a good part of your airtime engaged in irrelevant thoughts.

Powerful, persuasive expression doesn't mean being redundant. Important points may be repeated, but the main ingredients are getting to the point, supporting it, summarizing, and concluding. Power does not come from being long-winded — at least not in the United States.

For those people without a Commanding style, this poses a considerable challenge. The Logical wants to explain her reasons. The Inspirational hopes others will be enthralled by her words. The Supportive thinks about the opinions of others and their comfort with her decisions. Each of these styles requires encouraging people to be happy with a plan, and that takes time.

For noncommanding women, the challenge is even greater than it is for men. Living a subordinate role, women have learned how to explain and excuse disagreements, rather than confront men with them. People interpret such explanations and excuses as revealing a lack of confidence and an inability to exert power. While women may view such actions as ways to persuade, men often see only the absence of conviction and power.

For those women who sense their ideas are being overlooked, one answer is to try getting to the point quickly and providing only essential, persuasive reasons. Strip away peripheral arguments; mention only those that provide the strongest support for an argument. *Get rid of claim clutter* — the arguments and explanations that detract from your position more than they add. Initial proposals typically benefit from brevity in the presence of clarity. It is usually possible to add further support later.

VERBAL SPARRING

Among the many forms of power is one called "referent power." People derive referent power from being perceived as similar to those who have power. This poses an obvious problem for women: We look different from most of those in power. We usually sound different as well, and few of us know how to engage in verbal sparring — a form of male jousting that strengthens interpersonal bonds when played well.

At a recent graduation ceremony, I stood beside two professors who were engaging in verbal sparring. The conversation went as follows:

Professor A: How did you like teaching this class?
Professor B: It would have been better if you hadn't been around.
Professor A: Oh, you mean my stealing some of your thunder by using that case?
Professor B: Yeah. Pretty underhanded.
Professor A: You've got to be quick around here.
Professor B: I guess so.

This short conversation was punctuated by smirks, glancing rather than direct eye contact, and mutual chuckling. Professor B succeeded in communicating to Professor A that he was not pleased with his introducing to the class the same case Professor B planned to use later. Rather than apologize or explain his positioning, Professor A took the tone of Professor B's public attack to be an invitation to spar. From my reading of the situation, the conversation could have taken several tracks. Professor A opted to mildly one-up Professor B by accepting responsibility for adopting the case while also suggesting that he had outwitted Professor B by doing so ("You've got to be quick around here"). In actuality, both professors knew that Professor A did not purposely select a case that Professor B intended to use. But rather than say, "I'm sorry. I had no idea. I won't do that again," Professor A feigned intent to make Professor B's life difficult. In so doing, he avoids apology, diverts Professor B's anger into banter, but still conveys understanding of Professor B's feelings by categorizing his own use of the case as "stealing" from Professor B.

I've witnessed a number of women spar like this with men and with other women. They have learned to bypass cues that would normally elicit defensiveness, serious explanation, or apology. Verbal sparring requires lightheartedness. It is often quite full of meaning, yet does not invite long-winded responses. The correct retort to a verbal-sparring cue is cryptic, involving what was described in Chapter 2 as one-up moves.

Once, while taking my two sons to their swim lessons, I saw a male swim instructor approach another, raise his fists, and jump to and fro, like a boxer inviting the other to fight. They lightly punched at each other for a few seconds, then traded high fives. Replace the jabs and the high fives with words, and you have verbal sparring.

Women are often excluded from verbal sparring, yet they can become quite proficient at it. By doing so, they gain entry into conversations from which those who cannot spar are excluded. The precarious nature of verbal sparring makes it dangerous. There is always the chance of stepping outside the bounds and wounding someone. So invitations to spar from men to women are rare.

Here is an example of sparring I observed between a male investment executive and a female CFO while meeting with them at a restaurant. At one time the female had worked for the male. At the time of the conversation, they had moved on to different companies. The female had arrived a bit late to the restaurant.

Male: Glad you could finally make it.
Female: For once you're wearing a watch that tells time.
Male: This from the woman who is always late.
Female: Me? Late? I'm never late.
Male: What do you call arriving at 6:30 tonight?

Female: On time. What do you call it, Mr. Lateness?
Male: I'd call it late.
Female: You'll be late for your own funeral.
Male: They'll probably have to hold it up for you.

This kind of talk went on much of the evening and across many topics. Occasionally the pair would spar for the benefit of everyone present, inviting us to listen with sideways glances and comments like "Do you believe this?" or "Let me tell you what she did one time."

The CFO's ability to spar developed on the trading floor of a large bank, where she had been the only woman. As a consultant there, I had observed firsthand how the men verbally accosted one another on a regular basis. Sometimes it got out of hand. There were a few members who truly did not like each other, and they would move quickly from verbal sparring into heated conflict. It was a tough kind of play — no place for the meek. They sparred close to the edge on many occasions. They were young and competitive. The market was in a slump. And it didn't take much to turn innocent banter into piercing barbs. To survive, the female learned to spar. She is now a CEO in a company where the sparring is not toxic.

Verbal sparring appears to be more gratifying to the participants as they get close to the precipice of relational decorum. Individual skill, company and division culture, and the extent to which the sparrers are observed by others contribute to the definition of limits. If a sparrer reads any of these incorrectly, the game is up — unless the other sparrer does a "save" and places the interaction back on its sporting track.

For women the challenge is greater. As one male senior public relations expert advises: "Women have to guard against the guy who feels trapped so he switches to sexual put-downs to win. He knows the woman isn't likely to resort to the same. It's not worth sparring with that kind of guy. He cheats." It's best to know your sparring partner before moving quickly. If you run into a person who resorts to sexual put-downs, your style will dictate your response. One cross-style recommendation from a female who spars regularly: "Smile, remain calm, and say: 'I see you got desperate, substituted crass for clever,' laugh a little, and bring the whole thing to a close."

In general, it pays to start small. Initially, spar lightly, as men do.

Remember also that while cleverness is necessary, winning is not. People who spar to the death eventually spar alone.

READING BETWEEN THE LINES

Part of power is knowing when what is said is not what is meant. For every boss who really means it when he says his door is always open, there are two who don't mean it. It's important to assess whether something is said just for show and when it is to be taken seriously.

"On the whole, women are not good at separating out fact from fiction at work," a male insurance executive told me. "I don't want to say they're naive, it's more that they are still learning the ropes. They haven't been burned enough or heard enough horror stories. Two times I've publicly contradicted our CEO, but most of the time I let things pass. When women come into the same meetings, they often think he really wants them to share their thoughts with him and to provide constructive criticism. They think he really means it when he says, 'I want to be kept apprised.' Most men know he means, 'I want to be kept apprised if what you have to tell me agrees with what I'm thinking.' You can tell him something contrary to what he is thinking if you make it sound compatible. It takes a while to learn this. And women often seem to be lagging behind, taking words at face value."

During communication sessions, women have often said, "If the boss is saying one thing and meaning another, he is dishonest." They ask, "Why should I have to figure out what he really means?" In a perfect world, you don't have to figure out what the boss really means. In this less-than-perfect world, words have both connotations and denotations. When a boss says, "I want your input," the denotative meaning of "input" — information feed — may not be what he has in mind. His connotation, or personal meaning for "input," may have nothing to do with constructive criticism. The ability to read between the lines requires familiarity with the connotative realm of the boss's communication. There is a big difference between a boss who lies and one whose meanings simply differ from your own.

MAKING YOUR SUPPORT COUNT

A former colleague of mine used to oppose the best of ideas. Almost invariably he argued vociferously against good suggestions. When conflict was about to break out, he'd say, "Okay, maybe I can go along with this plan, but just remember, I wasn't enthusiastic." Each time he acted this way, he was an instant hero. It struck me as manipulative, and one day I asked my colleague why he did it. He didn't seem surprised that I'd noticed the pattern. "It works," he said. "It lets me air my reservations, covers me just in case things don't work out, and makes everyone feel great when I go along."

While this is an example of manipulative behavior, it demonstrates that there are ways to increase the value of one's cooperation. Unfortunately, women too often lend support and too readily provide help for others to view their cooperation as valuable and hard-won. Indeed, there can be negative power consequences from easy accessibility and ready support. In a 1980 *Harvard Business Review* article entitled "Management Men and Women: Closed vs. Open Doors," Natasha Josefowitz described a study of 68 male and 102 female managers, where she found female managers twice as accessible as their male counterparts.[19] There are, of course, positive consequences of accessibility, such as remaining in touch with employees, being sensitive to subordinates and helping them improve, and detecting conflicts before they get out of hand. But the ever-accessible manager loses valuable time, risks overloads that lead to poor performance, and robs subordinates of the ability to figure things out on their own. Worst of all, constant availability may send a message that a woman doesn't have any important work to do. Power can be undermined when a manager does not value her own time enough to be selectively accessible.

For women to gain power, they must be available for opportunities that can bring them the best returns. This does not mean refusing to mentor or dropping all altruistic behaviors. It means recognizing and responding to the natural human tendency to want and value what we believe is scarce. Research by psychologist Jack Brehm has demonstrated that whenever free choice is limited or threatened, the need to retain our freedoms makes us desire them more. In his book *Influence,* Robert Cialdini borrows from this research to explain how creating the impression that something is scarce causes people to want it more. This "scarcity principle" of influence works with people as well as objects. When women are too accommodative, they create the impression that their time is not scarce. They inadvertently diminish their own power.[20]

Creating the perception of time scarcity requires setting some hard-and-fast rules about the use of time. First and foremost, every woman who wants to increase her power needs to learn to say no. When someone suggests a meeting for a certain date, agree only if it is truly convenient. "That's not good for me. How about Thursday at three o'clock?" is easy to say once you believe your time is valuable. Another option: I can meet then but only for one half hour.

Stephen Covey, author of *The Seven Habits of Highly Effective People*, advises learning how to say no without offending. One of his experiences demonstrates how a no answer can be presented in a highly palatable manner even to a supervisor. Covey requested that a young employee do some work on an urgent matter. The young man replied, "Stephen, I'll do whatever you want me to do. Just let me share with you my situation." He then took Covey over to his wallboard, where he went over a list of two dozen projects he was working on, including performance criteria and deadline dates that had been negotiated earlier. He then said, "Stephen, to do the jobs that you want done right would take several days. Which of these projects would you like me to delay or cancel to satisfy your request?" Covey gave the urgent job to someone else.[21]

No doubt there are bosses who don't care how many jobs you have on your plate. They want them all done right and on time. But most bosses realize that expecting too much of good people only leads to mediocre output. The young man in Covey's story learned early that there are ways to say no that do not alienate others. For those scoring high on the Supportive dimension of the LSI, it is difficult to say no if doing so may cause offense. For Supportives, it is especially useful to practice ways of declining that are relationship enhancing. My colleague Alan Rowe advises that Supportives have within their response repertoire such phrases as "I'm very pleased that you asked me, but I will be unable to help out that day" and "Thank you for offering me this opportunity. I'd grab it in a minute if I could, but . . ."

KEEPING IT BRIEF

Deborah Tannen, in her book *You Just Don't Understand,* discusses how men and women think about talk. To men, talk is for information. But to women, talk is for interaction. Women don't neglect information, rather they include it within their "interaction" talk. They provide details and often elaborate on information in ways that are foreign in traditional male-dominated organizations.[22]

"A woman works for me who is really bright," a manager told me. "Her only problem is that she blathers. She doesn't seem to be able to control it. The men look at her like she just landed. They tune out. I'm sure she thinks that all the details she provides are important, but that's not how men see it. They just want her to get to the point. Usually she gets herself into a mess by giving them too much information; stuff they use later."

There are men who blather. They too pay the price in terms of promotion. There is a common perception, though, that women do so more often. To contradict this impression, women need to consider their audience. If detail is required, it may pay to say, "Bear with me for a moment while I give you a little background." It's usually better to be brief, to hit the strong arguments hard. As one successful female senior manager of a New England financial services company told me, "The senior vice president has said more than once about me: 'You have to watch her. She is quiet. But when she says something, it's important.'"

THE ELEMENT OF SURPRISE

Power is rarely predictable. A fifty-five-year-old female marketing vice president who attended one of my seminars told me this is where women lose some ground. "They allow themselves to be open books. You can't do that. You have to be somewhat unpredictable. Otherwise they can play you like a piano. If you're always defending one type of issue, or if they know your Achilles' heel, you're dead. It's important to occasionally help out when they expect you to be a roadblock. Then you keep them guessing."

One of the better examples of this was told to me by the editor of a paper products company in-house magazine. "I'll never forget when one of our best magazines had been released. That day a senior v.p. called me. He started yelling and screaming about how we'd misrepresented his division. He said the numbers in one of the articles were all wrong. He carried on about our ineptitude and threatened never to let any of us into his area again. He was just plain wrong. We'd checked the figures twice with his assistant. He hung up the phone before I had a chance to tell him that. I was steaming when I walked into my boss's office. I told her the story. She listened, paused, and said, 'Send him a rose.' 'A what!' I said. I had a host of other less appealing things on my list of things to send him. She repeated, 'Send him a rose. Not a real rose. Send him a memo. Tell him how much we value working with him. Explain to him our policy of checking all numbers. Let him know we did that in this case, but don't dwell on it. Explain that we will issue a correction in the next edition of the magazine. Let him know that the most important thing to us is continuing what has been a very positive relationship.' I had my reservations to be sure. But I did as she suggested. Some weeks later I saw the v.p. in the hall. He walked up to me, shook my hand, and said, 'I like working with you.' That was all he said. It was enough. Apparently he likes roses."

The moral of this story is that responding in ways people do not expect can prove useful. In conflict situations, it can reduce antagonism. In his book *Influence,* Robert Cialdini describes reciprocity as a fundamental form of human interaction. Think about what happens when you're furious at someone and they walk up to you and say, "I really blew it, didn't I. What a jerk I was." The typical reaction is to feel less angry. When people put themselves down, we reciprocate by raising them up. If they place themselves too high, the tendency is to pull them down. When people are poised for attack, consider offering an appeasement.[23]

I was the beneficiary of this doing-the-unexpected strategy in a recent conversation with a university administrator. Only a few weeks earlier he had replaced another man with whom my relationship had been rocky, to say the least. Our styles had been at cross-purposes, our views of the world from entirely different angles. When I entered the new man's office, I half expected the same treatment from him. After all, I had forewarned myself, the two men had known each other and worked closely. Only a few minutes into our conversation, he said, "I want to tell you something." He looked directly at me, waited until I was returning his gaze, and calmly said, "Whatever unpleasantness there might have been between you and my predecessor is over now. You and I are starting from scratch." For a moment I retained my focus on his expression. He smiled slightly, but the look of sincerity remained. He continued, "I'm a tough guy to please." I'd already heard that, so I said, "Yes, I know." He nodded, raised his hand to interrupt our mutual train of thought regarding his high expectations, and added, "But I respect competence and I'm not cold-hearted." At the close of our conversation, I left his office knowing the jury was still out on the future of our working relationship, but he had surprised me. I'd become accustomed to negativism from the man he'd replaced. By not adopting that style, this man had removed several stones from a wall not of his making.

INFILTRATING

A significant form of power is knowing the right people. This often means being able to network and infiltrate. My favorite infiltration story came from a ninety-two-year-old retired female insurance sales-person and broker. She is now a philanthropist. Her name is Mathilda Spak. When Spak was eighteen years old she decided to get a broker's license. Her only problem: She was too young. The law required that brokers be at least twenty-one. "I got one of my aunts to tell them I was twenty-one. I got my license. But I soon learned that no one wanted a female broker. The Chicago Broker's Club wouldn't even let women in. I decided that wasn't going to stop me. I became a secretary. Each day I'd have to enter through the alley door of the club. Women couldn't go through the front door. I listened and worked for as long as I needed to become quite a knowledgeable broker. Then I quit. The knowledge didn't seem to be doing me much good though. As soon as someone heard me say, 'My name is Mathilda,' they didn't want to do business. I decided to go into selling insurance, but it wasn't any easier there until an old lawyer friend of mine said, 'Don't call yourself Mathilda Spak. Use your middle name and first initial. Call yourself

M. Karel Spak. And your company should be M. Karel Spak Associates. I didn't have any associates, but it sounded good.

"To make a long story short, I got some great clients. I was the insurance agent for Equitable Life for twenty-five years. They never knew that M. Karel Spak was a woman. Then one day they called to tell me I would be receiving an award for my twenty-five years of service to their company. The award was to be presented at the Chicago Broker's Club. I called back to tell them that my company couldn't accept the award because women couldn't enter the club. They asked, 'What about Mr. Spak?' I told them, 'There is no Mr. Spak. Never has been.' That floored them."

Mathilda Spak was and still is a determined woman. She has spent ninety-two years learning the ropes. Gender did not stop her from acquiring the expertise she needed to succeed. This is what infiltration is all about. It requires ingenuity, determination, and, as in Mathilda's case, extraordinary actions.

Contrary to common wisdom, widespread infiltration is less effective than selective infiltration. Often people wanting to make the "right connections" reach out to anyone with power. There are two problems with this. First, doing so is ingenuous and likely to appear so to the powerful person. Second, it is often more expedient to form fewer, stronger ties than multiple weak ones. Management researchers Daniel Brass and Marlene Burkhardt differentiate between central and peripheral network positions.

> People in central network positions have greater access to, and potential control over, relevant resources such as information. People who are able to control relevant resources and thereby increase others' dependence on them are in a position to acquire power.[24]

While common wisdom supports a the-more-the-better approach to network contacts at work, Brass and Burkhardt found that this is not always an advantage.

> For example, an employee with a direct link to the most highly connected person in the communication network may have easy

access to important information without having a great number of contacts.[25]

The lesson here is that making contacts is less important than making the right ones. And surprisingly, the right ones are not always the people with visible power. It is not only important to connect with people who have information, they must be people willing to share it.

TAKING THE MEETING NOTES

Contrary to common wisdom, note taker can be a powerful position. A female manager from a Fortune 500 company told me, "Early on I avoided note taking. If the boss asked at a meeting, 'Who would like to take notes?' I'd say, 'You don't want me to do it. My handwriting is lousy.' That always got me off the hook. And I think in the beginning it was a wise move. But now I do take notes often. I've achieved high status in this organization. They aren't going to think I'm the secretary if I take notes. And I find that note taker is a position of considerable power. The person who takes the notes gets to write down what is said in ways that emphasize what they find important. You have to include everything, but within reason, few people begrudge the note taker putting his or her own twist on the proceedings. I find it is an important thing to do in meetings in which ideas important to me will be discussed."

This is one of those counterintuitive strategies. Most women avoid note taking at every turn. Here is a woman who makes quite clear the value of having the official pen in hand. It's a surreptitious means of shaping reality. As such, it can be a very powerful job.

THE POWER TO DELEGATE

If you clean the house before the cleaning person arrives, you're likely not good at delegating. If you are convinced that no one can do the job as well as you, then you also could use some remedial delegation training. And if you refuse to delegate because it might upset the person you're asking, the same is true.

Nobody can do everything. Everybody knows this. But many people, especially women, don't like to delegate. For women a reluctance to do so can be traced to our earlier discussion of women's discomfort with hierarchy. A preference for relational equity makes it difficult for them to use status as a reason for assigning others projects they themselves do not want to do or have no time to do.

The woman manager of the 1980s followed a superwoman model. She was supposed to bring home the bacon, fry it up in the pan, and still have time to swoon over her man. There is no doubt that this model continues to have its influence. But it's dangerous for women's success and their health. The only way to survive in an information age, when project demands can traverse the country faster than people, is to delegate.

The key is to match projects to talents, to stretch the people who want to be stretched, to be willing to share the credit, and to reward people when they get the job done. Each of these is a commonsense rule. But it is surprising how often they are overlooked. Delegating is made all the more difficult when people are asked to do things they believe are beneath their abilities. If they must be asked, they should be told, "This job is a no-brainer for you, Sharon, but it would mean a lot to me if you took it off my hands." Most people want to be helpful. They don't enjoy a steady diet of menial tasks, but they'll take several on if they know it is making a contribution and that it is appreciated.

Once again it's important to develop ways within your own style of comfortably doing what is usually uncomfortable for you. In terms of delegating, the following style-specific options are examples:

THE COMMANDING: "Here's a challenge for you. It has to be done today."

THE LOGICAL: "There are many things we need to accomplish, but this is at the top of the list. Since you have the skill to do it right, I'm giving it to you."

THE INSPIRATIONAL: "This may seem a small task to you, and perhaps an aggravation, but to me it's an important paving stone in our path to a much bigger payoff for all of us down the road."

THE SUPPORTIVE: "There are a lot of people who could do this, but it has to be done right. I'm counting on you. Thanks."

A FEW MORE WORDS ABOUT POWER

The way power is played and displayed varies across organizations and their divisions. It does women and men less good to learn the ways of one organization than it does to learn the varied ways power is expressed. Taking this learning a step further, the real benefit comes in experimenting with some of these forms. Doing so achieves what Rosabeth Moss Kanter describes as transferable knowledge that may be used across situations within a single company or brought along to the next job.

The main message of this chapter, though, is that power is often more perception than reality, more a way of acting than a way of being. Power doesn't just come to people, especially transportable power in the form of skills and expertise. Women must be willing to experiment with power, to infiltrate, delegate, manage their accessibility, and move beyond preferred styles of communication that limit their options. This is not the same as learning to be like men. It's also less about pleasing male superiors and bosses than it is about acquiring a personal communication mastery that cannot be taken away. This is transportable power.

|| 7 ||

WHEN TO TALK, WHEN TO WALK

"WHITE, MALE & WORRIED" read the cover story of the January 31, 1994, issue of *Business Week*. Men are becoming increasingly threatened by women competing with them for jobs, explained authors Michele Galen and Ann Therese Palmer.[1] The result is a "white, male backlash." At the heart of the issue for many white men is the fear of losing out to women and minorities.

Add to this the growing fear that women might unfairly accuse men of sexual harassment or take offense at what many men see as harmless humor. The head of neurosurgery for a major research hospital exemplified this concern as he explained to me, "We have no women in our department and we're afraid to hire any. We don't want to have to deal with claims of harassment." He went on, "I'm very careful around female medical students. No joking, no additional sessions, no personal attention. It's too risky. I tell them what they need to know and that's it."

This increasingly common attitude faces women with a dilemma: Do we take steps to make men feel comfortable or risk being labeled a threat? How, for example, should a woman react when a man interrupts her to announce, "You're awfully cute when you're angry"? What should a woman say when a male colleague or boss asks how many men she slept with on the last company retreat? Women wonder how to respond to such incidents without losing the trust of male co-work-ers and without being branded "radical feminists."

Women who've had repeated experiences like these begin to wonder how long they can refrain from responding abrasively. How many in-sults and slights should they endure, they ask themselves, before giving back what they've been getting? Most have been advised to avoid con-frontations. "You catch more flies with honey," they've been told. While I've long been an advocate of resolving conflicts with as little loss of face as possible for everyone involved, there are times when this philosophy is contraindicated. Each of us is at least 75 percent responsible for how we're treated. We fail ourselves when we continu-ally let abusive statements or treatment pass unchallenged.

THE EDUCATIONAL VALUE OF "BEING BROUGHT UP SHORT"

I've learned in my personal life and profession that everyone needs to be brought up short now and then. Who among us is so emotionally and intellectually competent, so consistently perceptive, that we see things clearly and objectively all the time? Learning doesn't end with formal schooling. Why is it that women feel they must avoid upsetting men or confronting them? By failing to object to disrespect and disre-gard we rob them and ourselves. We rob *them* of the opportunity to learn; we rob *ourselves* of the opportunity to change our lives for the better.

As I thought about the title for this book, some people advised me to choose one that would not offend anybody, especially not men. People I respect encouraged me to tone down the "us versus them" implications of the title I chose. All this worry reminded me of the time that my then seventy-five-year-old Aunt Peg asked me why I'd chosen persuasion for the topic of my first academic book. I was not yet thirty at the time. "Why would a young lady write about such a thing?" she asked. Aunt Peg considered persuasion to be outside the bounds of feminine dialogue. Women were supposed to be subtle; they weren't supposed to admit to using persuasion; especially not in my aunt's heyday. But while my Aunt Peg may not have liked talking about persuasion, she certainly engaged in it. She didn't tolerate anyone pushing her around. At restaurants, she wouldn't even let the host tell her where to sit. She would select her own table. And, to my youthful horror, she took her sweet time about it. But Aunt Peg taught me to expect to be treated well. To demand it when need be. She had learned that people often won't treat you well unless they know you expect it of them.

There's a little of my Aunt Peg in most women. One part of us wants to be appreciated for our poise and charm. The other part wants respect. We'd like both to come without having to ask or persuade, and especially without having to demand. But there are organizational cultures that deny women respect for their ideas and accomplishments. In such situations, subtlety has often proven more a hindrance than a help.

Consider, for example, companies that engage in what Dr. Keith Russell Abdow, chief resident in psychiatry at the New England Medical Center in Boston, describes as "tests of faith."

> "In the dozen of back-room men's club gatherings to which I have been privy, no one has ever fully broken ranks with the group by strenuously objecting to the degradation of a woman."
>
> "The lack of vocal opposition is multifaceted. To many men, sexist remarks can read like tests of faith in that refusing the implied camaraderie will lead others to doubt their sexual prowess. Participating in this reduction of women to objects is offered as proof of manliness."[2]

In such organizations, the unstated rule of silent tolerance in the face of the disparagement of women only undermines women's progress. The man who defends women by saying, "That comment was uncalled for" or even "I think we'd better lighten up on the sexist comments" risks being branded an outsider. Women are similarly constrained. Their acceptance of disparagement and sexist comments is often born of a fear that they may be labeled "radical feminists." Women know this label can destroy their chances of an eventual invitation into the upper echelons of predominantly male businesses.

In environments like the one described by Abdow, it is silence — not feminism — that perpetuates the derogation of women. Piaget believed that violations of our expectations provide opportunities for learning. Being brought up short, as the saying goes, is a path to learning. If they refuse to allow themselves to be disparaged, women violate the expectations of men who have come to rely on their silence. It is only when women speak up and risk labels in favor of redirecting communication between men and women at work that real learning takes place. For men the learning comes in the form of a wake-up call. When confronted by a woman who will not accept being talked over, overlooked, or insulted, they learn to think before doing so again. For women the learning comes in discovering that there is no shame in self-protection. The real shame is in its absence.

WHAT COMES AROUND COMES AROUND AGAIN

No one can, or should, fight every battle. It pays to develop a system for determining when a derogatory remark exceeds your threshold of tolerance. When such a remark is clearly outrageous, a woman might say, "Don't say that again." This is particularly likely if the woman's style is naturally Commanding. A Logical might choose to explain the multiple reasons why the offender should avoid such actions in the future. She might say, "I can understand why you might think that way given your educational background and limited work experience with competent women, but it's still out of line." The Inspirational, on the other hand, would likely invoke higher goals and aspirations in attempting to raise the conversation to a higher plane: "With both of us desiring a cordial, cooperative, team environment, there is no place for a comment like that." The Supportive might encourage the offender to see the harm such comments or actions cause the relationship. One possible response: "You and I work well together, so what I'm about to say is a friendly suggestion. In the future, I'd appreciate your leaving remarks like the one you just made out of our conversations."

As Nancy Dodd McCann and Thomas A. McGinn describe in their book *Harassed,* women differ in their interpretations of what is sufficiently offensive to require corrective action. Researching one hundred women's reactions to potentially offensive events, they found that women realize that they cannot reform the world single-handedly or "rid the world of jerks."[3] Contrary to the myth that women are roaming about waiting to sue men, women allow a host of disparaging comments to pass because they know they cannot expect to succeed in male-dominated environments if they are forever fighting.

If a boss stops by a woman's office to comment about her recent business trip, "I'll bet you and Jim had a good time together. It must have been like a honeymoon," letting it pass is not advisable. Such comments require corrective action or they are repeated. The rule here is *What comes around comes around again.*

Depending on the style of the woman, the following are possible responses:

THE COMMANDING: "You've exceeded my threshold with that comment. I'll let it pass this time. Don't do it again."

THE LOGICAL: "When you said X, I thought you may have misspoken. But then you said Y. My interpretation of both these instances is that you are either attempting to undermine what I have to say or insult me. Which is it?"

THE INSPIRATIONAL: "Our relationship belongs on a higher plane than that. Comments like that undermine the kind of relationship we both value."

THE SUPPORTIVE: "Since we're friends, I'll be honest. That comment was offensive."

The relationship between the offender and the offendee as well as personal style enters into the selection of a corrective response. For example, each of us affords to those we like what E. P. Hollander has described as "idiosyncrasy credits." These are like money in the bank that can be used to pay for a bad relational moment. People essentially build up credits in relationships that can be used at times when they do something offensive.[4] This explains those times when women say, "He's basically a good guy, so I let it pass."

SEPARATING OFFENSE FROM INSULT

Whether to let a comment pass is an individual decision. It's important, however, to bear in mind that letting sexist or disparaging comments, whether outrageous or mildly offensive, pass sends a message of acceptability. My own rule is that there is a significant difference between offense and insult. Anyone is capable of accidentally saying something offensive, even to respected colleagues. If a comment is offensive, and the offender is informed of this, two things may happen. In the preferred scenario, he desists from further offensive comments and accepts the offended party's warning as a desire to protect the relationship. If the offensive behavior occurs again, however, it is no longer offense but insult.

Insult requires a stronger response or it will surely come around again. Even among friends, unheeded it may lead to anger, resentment, and even legal action (which reinforces the stereotype that women are waiting around corners, Title VII booklets in hand, for the remark that will launch them into EEOC complaints and lawsuits). If people develop ways of dealing with and preventing offensive remarks, the need for legal steps greatly diminishes.

I've not met a woman who longs to take legal action against her company or colleagues. The cost is too dear. The woman who complained in the Tailhook incident decided to leave the Navy because, as she explained: "The physical attack on me by the Naval aviators at the 1991 Tailhook convention and the covert attacks on me that followed have stripped me of my ability to serve."[5]

Most women want to correct the problems they face at work with as little publicity and ire as possible. What is lacking in most organizations is a sophisticated system for defining and dealing with sexually offensive comments and actions. Most large companies have sexual harassment guidelines and lengthy procedures for complaint, but few have considered the value of teaching people how to handle such incidents on their own. Few have truly committed themselves to ridding their corridors, offices, and factories of offensive comments and erased from their environment tests of faith for men and ready categories of radicalism for women who articulate their distaste for sexism. Often the responsibility for solutions has had to be turned over to the courts because prevention and early detection, so clearly vital to human health, have been ignored in health planning of organizations.

ONE WOMAN'S SOLUTION

Fran Silvers, member of a major U.S. bank's board of directors, has her own strategy for letting people know when they've insulted her: "I freeze them out with a stare. One not to be mistaken for hurt feelings. It helps to lower the glasses, peer over them, and without blinking rest your eyes on theirs for several seconds." Another option she's found useful is to say: "Is there some shortcoming in your upbringing that makes you think that comment was necessary?" She cautions, however, that she says these things in private.

According to Silvers, "There is a certain point where gentility ceases to be functional. Whenever possible, don't make people look bad. But if it's you or them, the choice is clear." Silvers believes that many men operate as though they have an "inherent right to comment on women." One of her favorite examples: "If you lost weight, you'd be pretty." One of her responses: "Wish I could stay and talk with you about that. Thank you so much for sharing it with me." When Silvers is interrupted, she responds by raising her voice and continuing to talk. But experience has taught her a more effective response: "You simply raise your hand — palm facing his direction — and say calmly but firmly, 'Your turn will come.' It isn't enough to merely say this. The hand signal intensifies the effect."

Silvers is familiar with being excluded. The bank was about to hire an investment banking firm. The chairman of the board of directors left her out of discussions prior to the board meeting. "This was not the first time I'd been treated like an afterthought," she explained. "So I went to see him. My comment: 'I know you couldn't have thought it through or you would have included me in the hiring discussions. You would have been more careful. But if you want my full support on this and in the future, I expect you'll remember to include me.'"

Fran Silvers's style is Commanding. She believes that saying things like "You hurt me with that comment" or "I was offended by that action" focuses the discussion on the woman, not on the offense. She believes in being clear. Sometimes, she admits, this approach stings. But finding sweet ways to inform someone of the error of his ways has not proven useful to Silvers.

When we spoke, Silvers was especially interested in ways to respond to what she described as the "You know what your problem is?" scenario. This scenario involves a man telling a woman why she isn't more successful. She provided an example from a conversation she'd had with Jack Wright, a peer with whom she had been working.

Wright: You know what your problem is?
Silvers: No. But I can't wait to hear.
Wright: No. I'm serious. Your problem is that you're just not deferential.
Silvers: I beg your pardon.
Wright: You heard me. Sometimes it's good to be deferential. You aren't.

As Silvers explained, "At this point in the conversation, I'm wondering what right he has to tell me this. What makes him think I have a problem, and who invited him to help me solve it?" I asked how she responded. She completed the interaction.

Silvers: Do you have the foggiest idea of what you just said? You just told the alpha wolf she shouldn't piss on the trees.

Silvers explained, "The alpha wolf tells the others who they can mate with, who can urinate when and where. But the alpha wolf marks his territory first by urinating on the trees." She readily admits that this kind of response is strategic. "First, I doubt he understood what I meant, but he figured he should know. Rather than ask, he just nodded and went away. He probably did some reading on alpha wolves after that. But he got my message. I was telling him that anyone with my experience and accomplishments shouldn't have to be deferential. It doesn't matter that I'm a woman. Besides, I haven't found that deference does much good. Courteous is fine. Supportive is useful. Deferential does not endure over time. And it isn't my style."

There are other ways to respond to "You know what your problem is?" scenarios. And Silvers readily admits that something other than accusing her of being less than deferential might have led to a different response. The question is: Why does this person feel he has the right to comment on my "problem"? If his intention is to be helpful, then the type of response Silvers used may be unnecessarily confrontational.

All of us can benefit from advice. If, however, the "You know what your problem is?" scenario was used to belittle or elicit anxiety, then responding in a way that discourages such exchanges in the future is useful. Silvers's method is one of many options.

GETTING PAST THE NOISE TRAP

Alan Rowe, a leadership expert and author of several books on style, believes that the outcomes of most disagreements and disputes can be determined early on.[6] He described to me a case where an employee had been seriously injured due to unsafe conditions in the shop. His fellow workers insisted the site manager arrange for new machinery and adequate training. Rather than fight, the manager told the men they were absolutely right. Not only should they have new machinery, he told them, they should have the best. He agreed with all their claims and assured them that he would take action to secure the new machinery. He added before closing that budget considerations were the only obstacle, but even those, he assured them, were secondary to the safety of the workers.

According to Rowe, the workers had gotten their answer, but they missed it. When the manager mentioned budget considerations, he was essentially saying, "We can't do this" while telling the workers he agreed with their reasoning and intended to take steps to rectify an intolerable situation. Most people — women and men alike — miss underlying messages. They fail to recognize that implanted in what seem agreeable conversations are hints that the requested action will not be taken. The manager's words — with the exception of the budget comment — constituted noise drowning out the real message. The noise served to protect him from direct confrontation.

I have found that women tend to be susceptible to the *noise trap*, especially when the noise includes relational comfort statements. Men are by no means immune to noise, but many have learned that the real message is often embedded in a larger, more pleasant one.

When a boss says, "Let's get a committee together to look more closely at that," it's wise to listen to whether he also asks for a report by a specific date in the near future. If not, he either manages poorly or has sent this idea into limbo. Likewise, when you're promised an answer by a certain date and the date is continuously extended, the real message may be that there will be no answer because you've already gotten it — and the answer is no.

I've seen many women waste valuable time by listening to noise when they should have been watching actions. Certainly there are times when a boss really does want a committee to study a concept more closely, and there are times when promised dates must be extended. But when such actions start to take on a pattern, it's usually a sign that noise is being used to soften the true message. The ability to recognize noise is helpful in the decision to talk or walk.

There are two basic ways to treat a superior who is a noisemaker: resign yourself to the fact that he does not intend to honor your request or make yourself a thorn in his side until he does. The first is emotionally challenging because it is hard to give up what we truly want. The second approach requires a willingness to take some risks in the form of follow-up memos regarding his promises and setting regular meetings to determine progress. It requires a sensitivity to the company culture. If memos are too threatening, frequent meetings may be preferable.

A more complex method I've seen work more effectively for men than women is to oppose the noisemaker in an open forum. This usually takes the form of a gentle reminder that you don't have to play by the rules either if there are no rewards in the system. I've seen this happen regularly in academe when a professor challenges a dean on some issue of importance. The professor doesn't overtly disagree, but may express some doubt about a proposal the dean has made. Those who have not yet caught on see this as a brave move, an ally of the dean disagreeing with him in public. But the act of bravery is a message — I'll scratch your back if you scratch mine. If the dean gets it, a week or two later the dean gives the professor an important committee assignment or announces that the professor will be assisting him in some important endeavor. The professor's public disagreement was noise. He cared little about the subject of the disagreement. He had used it to send the dean a message — be responsive to me or don't expect my wholehearted support in the future.

It's important to develop strategies for dealing with noise. Among them is refusing to allow the noisemaker to distract you from your goals while you wait to find out if he will ever respond to your request. Sometimes it may even mean finding a new job, if that is what it takes to remove a superior's power to make you miserable.

SOMETIMES IT'S JUST A BAD HABIT

"How much of the problem between men and women is just men doing and saying what they've done and said for centuries rather than any conscious intention to insult or devalue women?" a male psychologist asked me recently. Similarly, women often ask why a man whom they consider sensitive occasionally says or does something revealing either an underlying antipathy toward women or, they hopefully wonder, just a failure to think before speaking.

A considerable body of research supports the existence of what might be called the "It's just a guy thing" syndrome. At the heart of this syndrome is the reasoning that most men aren't aware of their offensive behavior because they are following rules that used to work before women became sensitized to sexist speech. Essentially, most men learned to speak in ways that many women have only recently come to deplore.

The language habits of the generation of men currently leading major organizations were developed back when women were more clearly an out-group. There is a human tendency to treat members of out-groups as if they are all the same. This tendency is called "out-group homogeneity." A second tendency is to derogate outsiders, referred to as "out-group discrimination."[7] In most major organizations, women still constitute an out-group. Since women have not reached senior levels in large numbers, they have been unable to break down the tendency for men to treat them as an out-group and communicate with them in ways different from the ways they communicate with in-group males.

While some men may purposely try to minimize the value of women with derogatory comments, sexual innuendo, and harassment, many slip into ways of communicating with women that are unsupportive merely because women are seen as an undifferentiated mass of out-group members. Thus male disparagement of women is considered more a function of out-group perceptions and language habits than of purposeful efforts to bring harm or insult.

Consider, for example, a compliment I received from a colleague whom I hold in high regard. He mentioned that a CEO with whom I'd been working was quite pleased with my work. As another colleague listened, he asked me to share with him the advice I'd given the CEO so he could improve his own persuasiveness. I was just about to thank him for his kind words, when he smiled at his colleague and added, "Of course we don't know how much of a role your charm played in the outcome."

Clearly, he was not used to complimenting women in the presence of other men without feeling the need to add a doubt phrase to reduce her value to that of other female out-group members. He was kidding, no doubt. But this kind of kidding is frequent and denigrates the professional value of women.

What should a woman say in such circumstances? She might say, "Only as much of a role as your charm plays in your success," "I believe it was more my brain than my charm," "Thanks for the back-handed compliment," or "Why did you say that? It ruined a perfectly good compliment." But most women laugh, let it go — and let it eat away at them for the next few hours or days.

Women who accept the "It's just a guy thing" syndrome as an excuse let such comments pass. Others take it upon themselves to foster change. They may use abruptness or clever retorts to return disparagement in the same disguise in which it was received. Some find a frank discussion of the problem more effective.

But for sure, the wrong solution is to laugh along with the covert disparager. It reinforces bad language habits, extends the life of negative stereotypes, and assures that what comes around comes around again.

MAKING UP FOR LOST TIME

In their book *Failing at Fairness,* professors Myra and David Sadker describe the different worlds boys and girls inhabit. Their research is an indictment of sexism in American classrooms that systematically denies girls many of the opportunities afforded to boys. The Sadkers argue that girls become second-class citizens through a process of denigration that begins to take hold in adolescence and continues into adulthood, placing young women at a considerable disadvantage by the time they enter the working world.[8]

One of the opportunities systematically denied to girls and women is the expression of anger. Carolyn Heilbrun's bestselling book *Writing a Woman's Life* is helpful here. According to Heilbrun, "Above all other prohibitions, what has been forbidden to women is anger, together with the open admission of the desire for power and control over one's own life." By being denied a voice that expresses anger, women are thereby also denied the exercise of power and control that frequently requires such displays. Women are thus relegated to a lifetime of marginality unless they break through a multitude of barriers, tolerate or ignore a host of derogatory labels, and admit to the desire for success and even power.[9]

The price for such women is often dear. Researcher Eleanor Maccoby found that a girl who maintains the qualities of independence and active striving, necessary for intellectual mastery and success, defies the conventions of sex-appropriate behavior and must therefore pay a price in anxiety.[10] Harvard psychology professor Matina Horner found in her review of research on male and female achievement orientation that "despite emphasis on a new freedom for women, particularly since the mid-sixties, negative attitudes expressed toward and about successful women have remained high and perhaps even increased and intensified among both male and female subjects."[11]

Paying a price for success is not reserved for women alone, but there are certain costs many women are refusing to pay. Instead, they are starting their own businesses and freeing themselves from hostile climates and glass ceilings. These women found that the price of success in traditional, male-dominated companies was greater than they were willing to pay. In many cases they did try to talk, but ultimately decided to walk. They tired of waiting for what Rosabeth Moss Kanter calls a "point of payoff" — when hard work's dividend takes the form of reduced work, more time with family, a sabbatical, or some desired reward.[12]

There must be a point of payoff for a talented, professional woman.

Sometimes that requires looking for another job. More often, I believe, it means recognizing that what comes around comes around again. It involves refusing to let noise drown out what really matters, recognizing and redirecting dysfunctional communication patterns, and speaking up when overlooked, interrupted, offended, or insulted.

The ability to change things for the better is typically enhanced by knowing you can walk. This is where garnering the power of human capital, developing skills for future use, is key.

This paid off for Susan Bartlett, who was offered a $250,000 salary by her company's key competitor. She called me shortly after receiving the offer. She had been with her company for sixteen years. She was attracted to the new job. But Bartlett liked a lot of things about her current employer. The CEO had made efforts to promote women, but few had broken through the barriers to the top. She thought the CEO's intentions were good but senior management's follow-up left something to be desired. As we talked, it became clear that she was in a rather powerful position. She had the skills to walk. She even had an impressive salary offer. I told her that she would probably not find herself in such a strong position to have an impact on her employer than she was in at the moment. We discussed what she might ask for in terms of salary, but mostly in terms of how the company might really improve the climate for women.

Two weeks later, I heard from Bartlett. She had decided to talk rather than walk. She and five other women who were considering leaving the company joined her. They talked with Bartlett's boss. He not only listened, he promised to let them provide direction in turning the company culture into one conducive to the advancement of women. He allocated the financial resources to do so. The CEO concurred and is meeting with Bartlett as well. Bartlett knows she can still go to the competitor if things don't work out. They've been trying to recruit her for some time. Her preference is to make a difference at her current company.

As companies downsize, rightsize, and reengineer, loyalty is taking on a new look. There is a "new career logic" involving loyalty to self rather than company, and commitment to tasks, not organizations.[13] It isn't so much a selfish logic as it is a form of self-preservation. In this climate, women cannot remain silent when deprived of opportunities.

There is no logic to silence in an environment where the job you have today could be gone tomorrow.

SUMMARY

Reaching a point where you know you can walk is not only personally empowering, it makes you more attractive to your current employer. People who have acquired enough skills, experiences, and wisdom to walk are the very people smart companies encourage to stay. Talking and walking are not mutually exclusive options. It is talk, speaking up, expecting the point of payoff, and refusing to be devalued in the process that make walking possible. Talking is what should make walking unnecessary. But if it doesn't, at least you've had your say, maintained your integrity, and learned some portable lessons in the process.

‖ 8 ‖

ET TU, BRUTE?

COMMON WISDOM INFORMS that women prefer to work for male bosses. That's the trouble with common wisdom; it is so often mistaken.

Long before women entered the workplace, long before there was any such animal as a career woman, there were disparaging stereotypes of women with power and of women who wanted to work outside the home. They were seen as selfish iron maidens who schemed and connived their way to power. A desire to succeed in business was considered antithetical to the more valued desire to be a lady. In 1986 I encountered this perspective just as I was to speak to a conference of international financial experts in Zurich, Switzerland. One of them asked me, "So, when you finish your speech and return to your country, what will you be? A business lady or a lady?" I smiled and replied, "In my country a woman can be both if she chooses." He smiled the smile of experience and said, "I have traveled the world and that is not true anywhere. Not even in your country."

My critic was from Saudi Arabia, where women do not engage in business with men. But it's not necessary to travel to Saudi Arabia to find this sentiment; it is harbored in the minds of many people. Women supposedly abandon the mantle of ladyhood (i.e., being a gentlewoman) when they become career women. Men are not seen as choosing between being businessmen and gentlemen.

This either-or image of women has lost some of its popularity as women have moved toward critical mass in management. Yes, women have found increasing acceptance as an integral part of American organizations, but few companies have vanquished their biases and not all employees see career and ladyhood as comfortably connected. Some people have ceased to care whether they are connected or not. Even so, women are no longer willing to abandon their femininity to get ahead. "They don't have to have balls anymore," a male entertainment industry manager told me. "But my female boss has them," he added. "She's always had them, so she can't shake them. She had to have them to make it in this business in the early 1980s. Now she's stuck with them."

Many women have made it to the top of male-dominated businesses by aping the male style. They "bested the boys" in their career focus, can-do management styles, and unrelenting self-promotion. And those women learned that men didn't want them to be men. Men wanted them to be competent but not arrogant, assertive but not overly aggressive, savvy but not superior. It seems as though men wanted to have it both ways: Women as men expect them to be, yet women able to fit in and pull their own weight. The contradictions in expectations were enormous.

The women who cracked through the glass ceiling and made it to senior positions in traditional industries or steamrollered their way into executive suites and held on tight found themselves under continuing scrutiny. They were treading on new territory and their every step was noticed.

Is it any wonder that more of these women have not stuck their necks out trying to get other women to the top? They've been too busy "mixing it up with the big guys." During the 1970s and 1980s, women who broke down barriers to entry at the top of traditional organizations found themselves elated but usually alone. They soon learned that not being a man still had its limitations. Many had learned to act like the men who acceded to senior management in their companies. For many the act went against the grain, and it took much of their energy to gain and maintain credibility.

Most successful career women of the 1970s and 1980s were neither selfish nor uncaring. They did not regard women below them with disdain nor did they take on queen-bee attitudes and mannerisms. Some may have played the male role to the hilt, but most were very busy learning the ropes and coping with constant scrutiny and a sense that their feet were not yet fixed. They were keenly aware that getting through the glass ceiling did not guarantee remaining there.

Today, women are moving away from such feelings and they are reaching out to other women. A 1993 *Working Woman* magazine survey indicates that most successful women are making special efforts to mentor other women. Sixty-five percent of the 2,250 respondents said they speak out for other women, and 75 percent of top managers reported being satisfied with their own efforts to help women. A significant number of middle managers, however, thought that many senior women distance themselves from women's issues. Most of these middle management women were in companies employing 250 or more people.[1]

It may be that the larger the company, the less likely it is that women will come to know each other. Or the fact that mentor relationships are more difficult to establish from a distance may be at the root of the middle managers' feeling that senior women are aloof. But one certain factor is that most companies don't reward or encourage women or men to mentor junior women. Since women often are left out of organizational networks, the absence of mentors and the seeming unwillingness of senior women to reach out to them can create hard feelings.

THE GROWING ABSENCE OF SOLIDARITY

While the size of a company can inhibit the development of bonds between women, there is another reason why women often feel disconnected: *Women are becoming more different from each other than ever before.* Never before have so many women been working outside the home. For centuries their primary role was family caretaking, and women were in that role together. They were sisters in the common effort to support their husbands and nurture their children. They differed in personality and ambition, but most of them were homemakers first and foremost, even the minority who worked outside the home.

When I was growing up, my mother was one of the few women in our neighborhood who worked full-time. She was a clerk typist for the Navy Department at Sikorsky Aircraft. Each night at dinner, my mother and father talked about the challenges and high points of the day. I learned a lot about work from those conversations. I remember, too, that my mother was surrounded by women at work. They were the workers; men were the supervisors. The women supported each other. They had their differences, but they were in it together.

Women are not "in it together" anymore. They have different goals, interests, and inclinations. Some want to be CEO; none of the women working with my mother even dreamt of becoming Sikorsky's CEO. Gone is the solidarity that came with being wives and moms connected by neighborhoods and schools and family ties. The only women I meet in my neighborhood are working or else they are rushing their children to play groups, gym classes, swim classes, mommy-and-me sessions, and preschool. Life is hectic, each of us is pursuing a different dream, and it often seems we don't have time to connect.

Add to this declining dimension of solidarity, the push away from feminism. Many women in their thirties and forties have been somewhat embarrassed by the more radical extremes of feminism. These women no longer — if they ever did — wish to identify with the label "feminist," so they deny it altogether. They hesitate to gather around the lamp of feminism, despite the gifts it has provided them. What is left? Individual pursuits. The result? Our differences are now greater than our similarities. Women no longer share the same concerns and grocery stores. We have ceased to be reliable soulmates sharing the thrill of a new household appliance or the pursuit of a common cause. The paths we may take are incredibly varied. Life for us has become more complex than our mothers ever imagined.

Like the article mentioned earlier that attempted to divide women into the good mothers who don't work and the bad ones who do, much of what women read about each other is fiction. The whole idea of the "mommy wars" is ludicrous and insulting. It conjures up images of women duking it out over who is the best mom. Don't get me wrong: Many women who work worry whether they are devoting enough time to the children, and many women who do not work wonder if they should be working, or whether the time they are giving their children is adequately preparing them for school. The pressures are greater now than they were for our mothers. We now read a lot about child rearing. There are different schools of thought and every chance that you've subscribed to the wrong school. Stay home or work, few women escape the feeling that perhaps they have not learned enough about children's needs.

Vicki Whiting, a Ph.D. student who was about to have her second child, told me, "My mother never read books about how to raise us. She and my father just did their best. My mother doesn't understand why I need so many books just to realize that Phillip is doing what two-year-olds do."

Women are pulled in many directions, and we expect a lot of ourselves. My doctor tells me our bodies weren't made for the stress. But morbidity statistics on men indicate that they're not up to it, either. The important thing to realize is that none of us has all the right answers. We're doing different things, meeting different goals, and the best we can do is realize we're in new, uncharted territory. We are pioneers.

If working women bond on anything, it should be on a refusal to allow others to foist guilt upon them. There is a lot of room for guilt if you let it in. The house is never perfectly clean. The children may occasionally go to school with an imperfect lunch. You may be late to a meeting. But none of these things is the end of the world. And they do pass.

A case in point was the last day for submitting gift-wrap orders to my son's school. The gift-wrap sale was a big fundraiser, and there had been several reminders. Somehow, I had forgotten to send the order in to school with my child. How could I have let the date slip by? What kind of mother would do that? I pondered the awesome implications. I shared with my husband my failing, and then quickly corrected myself by referring to it as "our mutual failing." His reassurances fell on deaf ears. I knew in my heart of hearts that our son must be the only child whose parents had not returned their gift-wrap order on time. That night I once again burdened myself with my shortcomings. I was determined to turn over a new leaf. I opened my son's backpack and removed his folder, planning to read the contents and follow directions to the letter. Tomorrow would be a better day. I opened the folder. Before me was a most miraculous note: "Attention: Gift Wrap Sale Extended Until Wednesday 2:30 P.M."

The joy! The relief! The angel of gift wrap had granted our family a reprieve! What more could one ask? I shared the good news with my husband, who seemed less than moved. But I pushed aside his indifference. This was a victory of great proportions — a chance to be a parent who gets it right.

The next day I got my gift-wrap order in. By then, I was beginning to realize how much time I'd invested in self-recriminations. I promised never to do it again. After all, I reasoned, "I love my children. I do my best. I'm very busy. I can't be torn up over these little things." But I will do it again. Most parents I know will do it again. It's in the job description.

HIGH EXPECTATIONS FOR SENIOR WOMEN

The pressures on women to do all things well are enormous. The good news is that most are finding ways to make it work out. It's called time management. Finding good help. Sharing child-care responsibilities with spouses. Learning to live with dust. But women have a way to go with regard to cutting each other a little slack.

We've established in earlier chapters that women tend to focus on relationships more than men do. The female founder of a Los Angeles all-female film production company believes that "women are more circular than hierarchical in work relationships. They support each other in ways foreign to men. Women solicit opinions before formulating their own, and they share the work and the credit."

It is this same attention to relationships, however, that can create tension among women working together. Women expect other women to care about them as individuals. They expect some sensitivity to their concerns and receptivity to their requests. When a woman does not deliver these to other women, she may be perceived as cold or indifferent. The general consensus among women with whom I speak is that men get away with a lot more. No one expects men to manage and be sensitive too. When they are, they get a lot of credit. Women are supposed to be sensitive, and when they aren't, they are often criticized. This makes being a manager doubly difficult for women. They must manage people and help turn a profit, but not without spending time on nurturing and sympathizing. It can be very draining.

"I have to catch myself now and then from responding negatively to a woman because she isn't supportive," a colleague told me. "I shouldn't hold women to a different standard, but I do. When I was a kid, we combed each other's hair, we baby-sat each other's dolls, and we shared secrets. There was no hierarchy, no need for management. It's hard to break out of the mode of thinking that every woman ought to be caring and considerate. It means we can't be individuals."

The *Working Woman* survey found similar reactions: Fair or not, women have high expectations for each other. Senior women needn't take on every "woman's issue." That can damage credibility. But women do expect women to be fair and concerned about female advancement. It isn't enough for a woman to make it on her own. She has to be focused on both her own career and those of other women. This is not easy when everything she does is under scrutiny. It's hard enough to get work done and get ahead while being watched to see whether "women can take the heat." Add the expectation that women will find time and energy to mentor other women and serve on committees focused on women's issues. It pulls them in many directions and, in many cases, contributes to the stalling of their careers.

These demands take a toll. Whether in business or academe, women who forge the path are often tired. If they are not good time managers, they undermine their own careers and thereby contribute to the illusion that women cannot make it in the big leagues.

According to a recent Cornell University study, women experience considerable job stress. They make more personal sacrifices. For example, male executives are twice as likely to have children. According to Cornell's Dr. Timothy Judge, "In the push to the top, it seems that female executives are willing to absorb significant work/family stress in return for holding executive positions."[2] This is one of those areas where women can be of considerable help to each other. We must stop thinking that it is all on our shoulders. And we must advise each other to use our time wisely. This does not mean saying to a female colleague, "You do far too much," and then asking her to do more for you. It means recognizing that women are facing problems together and that the burden should be shared. Our tendency to nurture can lead to doing all the work. Women who make it to senior levels are leaders. As such, they are used to doing a lot themselves. But with leadership must come the ability to delegate. Without this skill and time management, we allow systems sluggish or resistant to female progress to win in the end. Why? Because when the sun rises on the battlefield, few women are left standing.

For a while you may be able to convince yourself that being a woman isn't an issue for the competent. If you're good enough, you tell yourself, you don't involve yourself in "women's issues" and that takes care of the problem of tiring yourself out. But let me say this from experience: They've got you where they want you then. They know you're afraid to allow any inkling of your femaleness to be noticed. You want to be one of the boys. Trust me, it doesn't work. And while you're lying low, other women are fighting your battles for you.

WHOSE RESPONSIBILITY IS IT ANYWAY?

Ask Xerox chief engineer Nancy Johnson whether she feels that women expect senior women to help them succeed and she'll tell you this story:

"There is an expectation that women at the top will move all women up. Many women who come in to get my advice want me to tell them exactly what to do. At first I did that. After all, I had a clear view to the top. I knew what I'd done. But I have quit providing this information. There were too many disappointed women. I now know that they can't get to the top the same way I did. I was a pioneer. Pioneers always do things weirdly compared to those who follow. Times have changed. The routes have changed.

"This story proves it. When I first came here as a marketing manager, all of my peers were male. They had a rule that women could not make long-distance telephone calls. Whenever I needed to make a call, the female operators would refuse to put me through. They essentially took my privileges away even though they were subordinate to me. Women below me in rank exercised control over a part of my job. They insisted upon calling my boss to get permission for me to place a long-distance call. In marketing, you have to be able to use the phone.

"The women joining the company today are entering a far different world. There may still be issues, but they can use the phones. The expectations and opportunities have changed. So, while I can provide advice, I can't tell them to do things the way I did. It won't work.

"There is another side to this as well. Some women think that I can make things right. That's not my job. I spend time with women. I tell them what questions to ask themselves. I offer guidance. My door is open. But my job isn't to get other women promoted. They have to earn it. I never signed up for that responsibility. I'm not their mother. It isn't that I don't care. It's just that my style is to help people who are promising whether they are male or female.

"One time a woman came into my office. She told me, 'I think I want to be a manager.' I said, 'Go home. Sit down. Ask yourself: "Do I think I want to be a manager or do I *want* to be a manager?" You have to know. It isn't a matter of feeling inclined.' That's the kind of advice I can give. I can't make everything all right. And I can't get anyone to the top who doesn't belong there."

I asked Nancy Johnson whether she believes that senior women think to themselves, "I made it to the top. I suffered. You can do the same." She paused and replied. "I can see how women would think that. I don't feel that way. But it would be easy to slip into that mindset. We should guard against it. No one makes it in this business entirely on their own."

Shirley Peterson, vice president of Ethics and Business Conduct at Northrop Grumman Corporation, agrees. "That is exactly why I do feel a responsibility to help junior women. I spend a good amount of time with them. I send notes offering assistance on projects. Some come in to get advice. If they're having difficulty communicating with a male boss or peer, we'll role-play what they might say. They find it helpful. Some have said, 'No one has ever done this for me before.' I'm always pleased to help an enterprising woman who knows she can learn something from people in my position. I've been there. I know the old boy network. Men helped me. Why shouldn't I provide the same to women?"

Peterson believes that women at top levels can and should be very helpful to junior women. "Margo, another female vice president, joins with me in recommending women for senior positions and high-visibility projects. If we hear that there is an opening in Finance, we'll recommend a woman. She has to be good. But that is no problem. We know a lot of highly competent women. It's just a matter of bringing them to the attention of the decision makers."

Peterson's attitude is different from that of women who believe that helping other women draws unwanted attention to their gender, that they'll be labeled "feminist." Peterson disagrees: "We don't mind drawing attention to our being women. We're straightforward about it. To some extent your credibility is on the line, so they have to be highly competent. But if you are thoughtful and insightful, you can select people who will do well."

If you ask Shirley Peterson what women seem to need help with, the conversation turns to communication and credibility. "Women are often shut out at meetings. After a while they pull back. They need to learn how to interject themselves into the action. In many organizations, men do a lot of positioning and posturing. That's how it looks to women. For women, it's like entering a boxing ring. It's a gamesmanship of sorts. When I complained about this to one of my male peers, he told me, 'It's all part of keeping each other sharp.' There are unwritten rules of the road. The people who survive are the ones who learn them and can work with them."

According to Peterson, women run less contentious meetings. They're more cautious about what they say. Women attend to fundamental considerations of organization, participation, clarity, time limitations, and closure. They come prepared to do a good job. They know they're being watched. They have a lot on the line. They've been shut out, and they don't want it to happen to people in their meetings. For a number of reasons, they facilitate groups better than most men.

One of those reasons is that women are usually more relationally conscious than men. They've not mastered the boxing ring style and are rarely adept at gamesmanship, so they make up for that by running a meeting in a way that gets things done. Part of mentoring junior women is training them to do this. Training them to get into the ring and mix it up with the big guys is useful, but men still aren't comfortable with that. Many men misinterpret women's intentions when they engage in behaviors similar to the men. Marilyn Loden describes this phenomenon in her book *Feminine Leadership*.

> The basic concept of women managers adapting to masculine norms contains its own catch-22. When all is said and done, regardless of how adaptable some may be, women are still women. Even when they attempt to behave exactly like their male counterparts, they are still not perceived by others in the same light.[3]

Below are excerpts from Loden's list of catch-22s:

How to Tell a Businessman from a Businesswoman
- A businessman is aggressive; a businesswoman is pushy.
- A businessman is good on details; she's picky.
- He loses his temper at times because he's so involved in his work; she's bitchy.
- He knows how to follow through; she doesn't know when to quit.
- He stands firm; she's hard.
- He is a man of the world; she's been around.
- He isn't afraid to say what he thinks; she's mouthy.
- He's a stern taskmaster; she's hard to work for.

A few additions of my own:

- He has his priorities straight; she's just playing hard to get.
- He's a man of action; she is impulsive.
- He's a family man; she has too many outside distractions.
- He thinks before he acts; she can't make up her mind.
- He tells it like it is; she's too direct.
- He makes things happen; she's lucky.
- He has good ideas; she operates on intuition.

The truth is that when women act like men their behaviors are interpreted differently by both men and women. It takes years for women to learn how to blend their own styles with those of men. This is where the help of senior women can be very important. Shirley Peterson has met a number of women on the factory floor who have found what she refers to as "their place." These "seasoned women" are often first-line supervisors. They are accepted and respected. They may not be polished around the edges, but they have found a happy medium between their own styles and those of the men.

Shirley Peterson and Nancy Johnson represent two somewhat different views on the importance of women helping women. Peterson sees it as a responsibility for senior women to recommend junior women or they will be overlooked. Johnson is open to it but believes that some of her pioneering efforts won't work for young women because too much has changed. She thinks that women ultimately must forge their own paths.

It's important to note that the cultures at Xerox and Northrop are quite different. Xerox has made some inroads with regard to promoting women, and Northrop is just beginning to do so. At Xerox women may be able to forge their own paths without much assistance. At most traditional companies, so many obstacles stand in the way of female progress that assistance from senior women is crucial.

When women do make it to the top, however, who mentors them? As Shirley Peterson describes, "It doesn't get a lot better at the top. You have to have intestinal fortitude. And there are trade-offs. What's disturbing is that the grass isn't any greener elsewhere. Women are trading war stories. We're learning that getting to the top can be lonely and extraordinarily demanding."

Women who had the impression that they could stop fighting on a daily basis to prove their worth if they could reach senior ranks are surprised when life in the executive suite comes into clearer view. At the top there are even higher expectations and even more work. The differences between men and women at such levels are magnified. Senior women work side by side with men who came up through the old school, who don't get it and never will.

Getting to the top of organizations run by such people is difficult for women. It's still a man's world. You have to want to be there very badly, and you must be willing to watch your back, play the games, postpone parenthood, and talk the talk. For many women that's just too much to ask, especially if there are other options.

ARE WE STEERING EACH OTHER WRONG?

There is something to the adage "Advice is cheap." It is also often wrong. This is what Nancy Johnson feared when advising women. If the road signs have changed, the advice of a pioneer can send you off a cliff. There is some evidence, both research and anecdotal, that women are relying on old rules to play new games. For example, it's imperative that a woman have an impressive track record if she wants to be promoted to senior levels. But it's foolish to think a track record alone opens the doors. The female mentor who advises her subordinate to "just keep your eye on the ball and hit it out of the park" may be sending a junior colleague down the wrong path. Competence is only one key to the executive suite. Even if it gets you in, it won't be enough to keep you there.

According to one female senior advertising executive who works side by side with men on a number of corporate boards, "The men on these boards think they've changed, but I hear them talk and most haven't." She believes that it is taking women far longer than anticipated to reach the top in significant numbers because men still don't feel comfortable with most women.

Dawn-Marie Driscoll and Carol Goldberg's book *Members of the Club* is supportive of this view. They write:

> Penetrating and changing the comfort zone so that it welcomes all executives is a challenge, but a necessary one if women are to reach maximum effectiveness. The bad news is that the zone creates a culture (and in some cases, a set of professional rules) that impacts most negatively on women, excluding them from arenas of corporate, civic and economic power.[4]

Driscoll and Goldberg believe that the comfort zone is accessible to women, but not on the basis of competence alone. Being the best at what you do is not a guarantee of advancement.

Women are also steering each other wrong when they overlook their own network potential. It bears repeating that women often make efforts to appear disconnected from other women. They fear that their male co-workers will perceive them as being "up to no good" when they meet with other women. This is a sure way to close off a very important avenue to success. As University of California, Berkeley, business professor Karlene Roberts has observed, power in organizations comes from access to resources and information. It pays to be in the right place at the right time.[5]

Often people overlook important power avenues by assuming that linkages to highly senior people, those in the direct chain to leadership, are most important. Such people may be helpful, but a number of alternative paths to power and position also exist. Among them are people who appear to have little power in the traditional sense. They may belong to different divisions of the organization or even work for a competitor. Researchers have discovered that people outside the direct line of ascendancy in organizations can provide valuable information, opportunities, and resources. This is referred to as "the strength of weak ties."[6] Women have been overlooking each other because they have not paid sufficient attention to the strength of weak ties — the value they can have to each other with regard to information and support. This does not mean that networking with women is necessarily better than networking with men. But worrying that men might think less of you if you form communication links with other women cuts off an important avenue. Once again fear gets in the way of women's success. For those women who have felt the fear, it is difficult to get by it. They wonder, What if Jack says something to my boss and then they decide I'm not to be trusted? Others think, If I let people know that I have close ties with other women it will just remind the men I work with that I am a woman. First, if you identify with these thoughts, you are likely overlooking two facts: They don't trust you all that much anyway, and they don't need reminders that you are a woman.

Once again it is important to know how to respond when comments are made about meeting with other women for lunch. The following conversation demonstrates the wrong way.

> *Phil:* I see you've joined the female mafia, Susan.
> *Susan:* It was just lunch. They invited me so I felt I had to go.
> *Phil:* Oh, it's not an issue for me. I don't care who you have lunch with. I'm just wondering about Frank's opinion.
> *Susan:* I'm not likely to see those women for another year.

Susan has abdicated the definition of her lunch meeting to Phil. He recognizes that fact and has used his definitional rights to make Susan uncomfortable. As described in previous chapters, Susan has engaged in one-down (↓) responses to Phil's one-up (↑) moves. A better scenario for Susan is as follows.

Phil: I see you've joined the female mafia, Susan. (↑)

Susan: I don't blame you for being envious. They are impressive and, as you know, well-connected people. (↑)

If the conversation continues:

Phil: Oh, it's not an issue for me. I don't care who you have lunch with. I'm just wondering about Frank's opinion. (↑)

Susan: Frank isn't blind. He knows a power lunch when he sees one. (↑)

Women are beginning to realize that cutting off a growing segment of colleagues merely because men might think you are planning something behind their backs is not productive. It's time to stop worrying about being seen with other women in the hallways. Only last week I was talking with a female professor. We were standing at the base of a stairwell discussing her career aspirations. One of her male colleagues walked by. He slowed down, looked at both of us, smiled an "I caught you" type smile, and proceeded up the stairs. I've come to the conclusion, as have many other women, that worrying about such things is futile. It is also a very clever way to keep women away from each other, thus severing what can be important connections. In situations like this women should ask themselves, What is the worst thing that could happen? The smirker might report to other men that he saw you in the hallway talking with another woman and it looked like you were up to something. He might imply to others that you and other women are "banding together." It's important to remember that if this kind of childishness can be used to harm a woman's career, the climate of that organization will likely ruin it anyway — all the more reason to have made connections with people of both genders.

My father gave me a very good piece of advice when I was no more than twelve years of age. I remember it well, although I readily admit to having failed to apply it at times. He said, "If you let them know something bothers you, they've got you where they want you." He was right.

KEEPING YOUR EYES ON THE PRIZE

The stereotype of women not wanting to work for women is a diversion. Among the many things I've learned from my friendship with

Betty Friedan is that you can't make progress if you're frequently distracted by side issues. There is no substance to the view that women don't want to work for women. They may not want to work for some women, but personality is the reason, not gender. The whole issue is a diversion and it's false. Let's put it to rest once and for all.

The *Wall Street Journal* found that some women-run businesses "can be positively antediluvian when it comes to hiring or promoting women into management positions."[7] On closer scrutiny, however, it found that almost all the women-run firms that scored low on promoting women had been inherited by women who had never learned firsthand how difficult it can be to come up through the ranks.

Esprit de Corps, co-founded by fifty-one-year-old Susie Tompkins, has a management team consisting of 69.4 percent women. The company makes no special efforts to recruit women because of the 5,200 unsolicited applications received in 1993, 63 percent came from women. Who says women don't want to work for women. They do if the women they'll work for won't hesitate to promote them merely because they are women.[8]

Sara Lee Corporation found the same pattern. Women are attracted to companies that promote women. It started hiring women into high-level jobs during the 1980s rather than waiting for women to make it up through the ranks. In time women lower in the promotion ladder had proof that they could make it to the top.[9]

Add to this equation women like Jean O'Shea, director of marketing for a leading producer of male and female grooming products. She gets tired of being the only woman at senior management meetings, she told me. But she doesn't sit back and hope that it might one day change. "I feel that I have to be a thorn in their side, reminding them there are far too few women at the top." She sees herself as a willing pioneer but not a sacrificial lamb. "I've come too far to let it all fall apart now. I speak up. I no longer worry that they'll think I'm too concerned about promoting women. I am concerned and I'm not apologizing for it."

SUMMARY

Women's interests are more diverse than ever before. Nevertheless, there is a growing sense that those who work share a common ground.

This revival of camaraderie is a welcome change from the "Let's not sit near each other at meetings" school of thought, which has kept women from providing needed mutual support. Staying away from each other, not providing help with promotions, and fearing labels are traps. Men don't make it to the top of corporations without the help of other men. Women shouldn't assume they can do it without the help of other women. And most women are coming to that realization. It's time to stop worrying that conversing with female co-workers in the hallway might be viewed as conniving and scheming for promotions behind men's backs. It's time to do it right in front of them.

‖ 9 ‖

CHOOSING THE RIGHT
WORK CLIMATE

LEARNING TO SPEAK UP is key to women's success. So too is expanding your style, but even more important in the long run is knowing how to find a work environment that doesn't require credibility-saving efforts all day long. Ones that do may be good for learning some tough lessons, but you have to ask yourself if you want to work where the people in leadership positions are incapable of recognizing talent unless it's male.

There are thousands of academic and practitioner articles and books on leadership. By now we have a pretty good idea what effective leadership in the 1990s and beyond should look like. According to Gail Fairhurst's review of leader-follower research, the traditional view of leaders as "directors," "planners," and "controllers" has been replaced with "talk of leaders as 'coaches,' 'visionaries,' 'symbolic managers,' and even 'servants.'"[1]

Fairhurst's use of the word "talk" is key. Most organizations spend far more time talking about new forms of leadership than they do implementing them. They remain "mechanistic" in their ways of work. Control and conformity are valued. Decision making is centralized and people are given limited opportunity for personal discretion. Researchers have repeatedly found that mechanistic organizations elicit feelings of isolation, powerlessness, and alienation.[2] People perceived as different from the dominant group are considered threats to the status quo. In such organizations, acceptance of what we've called "worthy differences" is found more in talk than action.

Returning to Ann Morrison's advice (see Chapter 4), diversity must include integration, not simply an awareness of its value. There must be evidence of positive talk about diversity being translated into action or the talk means little. It isn't enough to have diversity seminars — there must be real efforts to reformulate gender codes. This requires changing the dominant communication scripts, what Mary Catherine Bateson terms "skilled reconstruction." It can't be a one-sided effort where women learn men's games or claim that women's ways of communicating are, after all, superior. True gender integration of the workplace requires that women and men meet each other halfway.

My research on leadership and negotiation coupled with personal experience has taught me, however, that meeting halfway requires that someone take the lead — the first step. In some organizations men do so. But it's rare. Since women are the ones for whom gender equality means the most, they must be the catalysts for change.

How to do this effectively is what this book has been about. Speaking up, refusing to be talked over, overlooked, and dismissed are important. But there is one more important factor to consider: *There is nothing to be gained from women wasting their time trying to change organizations that don't get it now and never will.*

In earlier chapters, you read about women who refused lucrative job offers to stay in their companies despite the absence of proof that women were valued. You read about women who postponed families until they felt firmly ensconced in management positions and women who spoke up on behalf of other women to assure fair treatment. They did so because they believed they could play a crucial role in the process of changing their companies into ones appreciative of women. These women identified people in their organizations with the power to make a difference and were able to get their attention. They broke through dysfunctional communication patterns, expanded their styles, and learned new communication strategies. They guarded against noise in the system and avoided claim clutter so they could keep their focus on the payoff — getting ahead.

By contrast, staying in an environment that will never change to accommodate women is a waste of talent. And I didn't want to end this book leaving the impression that knowing what's going on and altering gender codes is either sufficient in every organization or desirable. It's always best to work where you have a fighting chance to be recognized for your competence and promoted for it as well.

Alex W. "Pete" Hart, formerly of MasterCard and now executive vice chairman of Advanta Corporation, believes that there are places where "nothing you say or do changes resistance to women rising to the top." He's right. These companies may never get it. And it pays to do a little soul-searching about whether you are working in one of those places.

To help in this determination, let's return to southern California, where this book started. This time, though, the conference is one that occurred two years ago under the auspices of the Leadership Institute at the University of Southern California. One hundred and twenty experts on leadership gathered in Pasadena to discuss what leadership should be in an age of global competition, information superhighways, and both cultural and gender diversity. This one-day conference revealed for all present what it takes to lead an enlightened company, one that can survive. Much of what was said by the experts there is important to anyone determining whether her company is one that can change for the better or one stuck irrevocably in the past. Out of this meeting came a set of four criteria useful for testing the climate and promise of organizations for all employees, especially women. The following sections review these criteria.

CONSENSUS VALUED OVER DEBATE

With the emergence of such business practices as participatory management and employee empowerment, many companies have become concerned with consensus building. Consultants are brought in to train employees how to arrive at consensus in meetings — how to assure that actions have employee "buy-in." These efforts are often born of good intentions but just as often neglect the value of debate and conflict in the development of people and their companies.

Michele Hunt, former vice president for quality and people development at Herman Miller, Inc., and now director of the Federal Quality

Institute, agrees. At the Pasadena conference, she described how the emphasis on consensus over debate and end over process has gotten companies into trouble. In consensus-based organizations, intellectual curiosity usually cannot thrive because disagreement comes to be viewed as disloyalty. According to Harlan Cleveland, president of the World Academy of Art and Science and member of the Leadership Institute board, "Intellectual curiosity is the prime characteristic of the leader of the future." Cleveland believes that the concept of "leader of the future" must apply not so much to powerful individuals but more to groups of people. The world is too complex and the trends that drive us are too often in conflict for us to expect that one leader can know and do everything or that one way of thinking is sufficient to address our most pressing problems. Cleveland believes that leaders have to work to incorporate differences.

This cannot be achieved without an appreciation for conflict. Connectedness and harmony do not arise from people hiding their true feelings to create the image of consensus. More and more, the workplace is composed of people whose life experiences differ. More important than consensus is a healthy acceptance of debate and a willingness to listen and learn. For women wanting to reach senior levels of their companies this is especially important.

A climate of consensus is also one of fit and comfort. Women in consensus-based companies are often viewed as an out-group that poses a threat to consensus. Women neither "fit" nor elicit "comfort" because their bosses wonder whether they can be trusted to play along to get along. The company culture is devoted to the illusion of participation and agreement, not the reality.

Such companies are not good places for women who want to reach the top level of management. As we've discussed in earlier chapters, you can't get ahead if you're unwilling to speak up, but in consensus-based companies you can't get to the top if you do. So the question to ask yourself is whether your company is like this. And if it is, can it change? If not, your talent and your time are being wasted. You may be better off looking for a place where your options are not so limited. Companies where debate is at least as valuable as consensus are also the workplaces where women pose little additional threat.

CONTROL VALUED OVER LEARNING

We live in a time when companies are downsizing, rightsizing, stream-lining, and, in many cases, replacing hierarchical management with task teams. At the Pasadena meeting, Robert Townsend, former CEO of Avis, described such companies as "panthers, enlightened organizations of the future." But he noted that the "elephants will still be around," referring to those organizations burdened by hierarchies that do not facilitate productivity.

Charles Handy, author of *The Age of Unreason* and *The Age of Paradox,* pointed out, however, that hierarchy need not be a bad thing. There can be task hierarchies that draw people from a variety of status levels. In such organizations, the issue is not whether there is a hierarchy, but rather whether it exists to facilitate the functions of the organization or merely to protect people. Is hierarchy a way of keeping people in power or does it facilitate communication and effectiveness?

Frances Hesselbein, president and CEO of the Peter F. Drucker Foundation for Nonprofit Management, shared with conference attendees her view that it's best to work where "people see themselves as leaders, not as giants among pygmies." Thus it isn't so much whether there are hierarchies but how they operate that makes the difference in whether women will be valued. According to Mitchell Rabkin, president of Beth Israel Hospital in Boston, people are hardwired to build hierarchies in much the same way that robins are hardwired to build nests. The important issue for women is whether these hierarchies are built to accommodate only men or whether with some tweaking and some enlightened people at every level of the hierarchy women can reach the top in appreciable numbers.

There was general agreement at the Pasadena conference that hierarchy in itself is not the culprit. Alone it doesn't prevent effective leadership. Some companies run better with established hierarchies. Just as there is no single form of government right for all countries, so too there is no all-purpose way to lead. As Harvard professor Abraham Zaleznik proposed at the conference, "The goal is not to end hierarchy, but to make it work better." For women this has to mean hierarchy that is enabling, not stifling. There must be people along the way who do not fear working side by side with those who look and perhaps talk and act differently than themselves. Without such people hierarchy is merely a defense mechanism — a means of keeping others out. Such environments are not conducive to the success of women. If you're in one, it's best to move on.

Larraine Matusak, leadership scholar and program director at the W. K. Kellogg Foundation, believes in the importance of letting down the defense barriers to allow people opportunities to lead. "Each of us has a passion. Each of us needs opportunities and encouragement for expression of our passions as part of daily work." Matusak recommends that people who work together also "weave their vision together to assure commitment." Hierarchies that protect rather than encourage are death to passion. Such organizations ask their people to buy in to ideas designed by those in power. "The trouble with buy-in," Matusak explains, "is that people can just as easily sell out." When hierarchy is used to keep people in line, to assure power stays with a few people who look, talk, and walk alike, the result is a buy-in/sell-out environment where what counts is whose side you're on rather than the merit of your ideas. For women, such environments are stifling. It's best to move on to find a place where passion can evolve into a significant contribution, a place where people help talented others move ahead no matter their ethnicity or gender.

WORKING HARD PREFERRED TO WORKING SMART

Peter Drucker told the Leadership Institute conference guests that too often people are asked to work harder rather than given the opportunity to work smarter. He explained:

> The word productivity surfaced post WW II. But the world up to then, everybody including Marx, including every economist, every industrialist, had known that people could work long hours and people could work harder, but nobody had ever thought of people being able to work smarter.[3]

Working smarter means being able to relinquish old ways of doing things. As Marilyn Ferguson, author of *The Aquarian Conspiracy*, explains, always doing what you've always done gets you what you always got.[4] One thing that many companies continue to do is measure the quality of people's work in terms of how hard they appear to be applying themselves. In such companies, arrival and departure times are used as indicators of commitment to the job. While there is nothing wrong with expecting people to put in a full day of work, much more important is what they accomplish.

Companies where commitment is measured more by the time at which people arrive and leave than by what they accomplish are not the best places for women. The reason is not only that many women have family demands but that such climates are usually rigid and guided by antiquated views of employee loyalty. If, for example, getting into work by 6:30 A.M. and leaving after 7:00 P.M. is the way employees demonstrate ability, find another place to work. Life is too short. Move to a company where value is measured by contribution and commitment by reliability.

MANAGEMENT BASED ON FEAR, NOT TRUST

Richard "Skip" LeFauve, president of the Saturn Car Corporation, was in Pasadena too. "Leaders should teach and learn," he said. "People change only when there is trust, motivation, guidance, clarity, patience, practice, permission to err, and reward for success." This combination lives more in the minds of people who lead organizations than it does in day-to-day actions. Sidney Harman, chairman of Harman International, told Leadership Institute board members at a later meeting that at the heart of the problem is the fact that businesses are "populated by clones of business school graduates who know how to do only one thing and live in silent terror because they don't have the big picture." These people try to mold everything and everyone to their liking. People different from themselves elicit anxiety. Trusting, letting people err, and rewarding them for success, among the other suggestions LeFauve made, are not goals of people in fear. They look for people like themselves. The result is a group of people all limited in the same ways leading organizations that could benefit immensely from diversity of ideas and perspectives.

It's easy to see how an organization run by people in fear is not a good place for women. Although trusting everyone is as foolish as fearing everyone, and equally nonproductive, somewhere in between are organizations aware that complexity requires dependence on others. None of us can do everything well. But all of us can surround ourselves with people whose talents complement or extend beyond our own. The complexity of today's work world demands that we expect to need other people, including people different from ourselves. Power-oriented elites can no longer do all the thinking. Research by Michael Driver, professor of management at USC, and his associates demonstrates what Driver describes as a continued "breeding of elitism" in many organizations. "We keep selecting people for their quantitative abilities," he explains, "even though we know that the complexity of work today requires moving away from autocratic, elitist leadership to more integrative forms." According to Driver, women lean strongly toward this integration.[5]

In most traditional organizations, according to Driver, it is men who lean toward autocratic leadership. So women working in such places must ask themselves how long they intend to wait patiently to have their contributions welcomed and rewarded. There is much to be said for forging a path, exhausting as it may be. And women who expend the effort and time to help their organizations see the value people like themselves can bring deserve to be on a list of contemporary female business heroines. Without them, women would have fewer choices than they have today. The only caveat is that there is a difference between butting your head against a wall that shows some sign of yielding and giving yourself a concussion on one that shows no such sign. At some point in a career that has reached a standstill, women must ask themselves which wall they are up against and take the answer to heart.

CONCLUSION

Many disappointments in life come from a failure to manage expectations. Betty Friedan, Gloria Steinem, and the women who worked with them in countries around the world gave women in my generation and beyond a gift. We expected, however, that this gift would be enough, that our work was largely done. We have discovered that it has only just begun.

For those women who leave traditional businesses to start their own, the challenge before them is to avoid recreating under female leadership the kinds of work environments they left behind. For those women who stay in traditional organizations intent on fostering change, the ones who long ago discarded the outmoded nine to five attitude that measures commitment by length of stay rather than contribution and seeks to motivate people by fear, the path is still uphill. Change is never easy, even less so when power is not yours. But women are gaining power not only because of their increasing numbers in the workforce, but because they are becoming less willing to wait to be noticed. They are not picketing outside office buildings or marching on Washington, but one by one they are finding ways to be heard and heeded.

This book was written to help women who often find themselves in sparse company when attempting to change their organizations. It's for women like Lois Valliere, director of ultrasound for an East Coast medical organization, who now realizes "I used to stop in my tracks when my previous boss said, 'Lois, why do you always make a male-female issue out of everything?'" Lois doesn't worry about statements like that anymore. She now knows that much of everyday communication is a male-female issue and expecting the situation to change by itself is as unproductive as expecting to get promoted if you follow the time-honored advice "Keep your mouth shut and play along to get along." There is much to be said for listening and learning the ropes, but women are learning that when men "play along" if they do "get along" it's because they are men and the people deciding how far they get are men too. In such environments the wiser course is to listen and learn but also to play an instrumental role in managing how others communicate with you and you with them. As I tell my students, managers don't manage reality, they manage perceptions. If you do nothing to change perceptions that limit your options, you play along, but you get nowhere. If, on the other hand, you see your communication with others as a vehicle for success that needs regular tune-ups and skillful handling, the opportunities for change are at hand. There are those who argue that we are who we are and only the foolhardy dare tamper. But we are who we are becoming and only the foolhardy dare leave it to chance.

NOTES

Chapter 1

THE COMMUNICATION CHALLENGE

1. See Michael S. Kimmell, "What Do Men Want?" *Harvard Business Review*, November–December 1993, pp. 50–63.
2. Carol Gilligan, *A Different Voice* (Cambridge, MA: Harvard University Press, 1982).
3. Lynn Miller, Linda Cooke, Jennifer Tsang, and Faith Morgan, "Should I Brag? Nature and Impact of Positive and Boastful Disclosures for Women and Men," *Human Communication Research*, March 1992, pp. 364–399.
4. Betty Lehan Harragan, *Games Mother Never Taught You* (New York: Warner Books, 1976).
5. Margaret Hennig and Anne Jardim, *The Managerial Woman* (New York: Pocket Books, 1977).
6. O. C. Brenner, Joseph Tomkiewicz, and Virginia Schein, "The Relationship Between Sex Role Stereotypes and Requisite Management Characteristics Revisited," *Academy of Management Journal*, no. 3, 1989, p. 668.
7. Lori Bongiorno, "Where Are All the Female B-School Profs?" *Business Week*, December 7, 1992.
8. Diana Trilling, "Sexual Separation: Is This the Direction in Which We Are Heading?" *Newsweek*, June 6, 1994.
9. Patricia Aburdene and John Naisbitt, *Megatrends for Women* (New York: Villard Books, 1992).
10. Laura Mansnerus, "Why Women are Leaving the Law," *Working Woman*, April 1993.
11. Julie Amparano Lopez, "Firms Force Job Seekers to Jump Through Hoops," *Wall Street Journal*, October 6, 1993.
12. Ibid.
13. "Women in Management: the Spare Sex," *The Economist*, March 28, 1992.

14. Rosabeth Moss Kanter, *The Change Masters* (New York: Simon and Schuster, 1983), p. 33.
15. Ibid.
16. Ibid.
17. Ibid., p. 63.
18. Francine Blau and Marianne Ferber, *The Economics of Women, Men and Work* (Englewood Cliffs, NJ: Prentice-Hall, 1992).
19. Kathleen Reardon, "The Memo in Every Woman's Desk," *Harvard Business Review,* March–April 1993.
20. Ibid.
21. Ibid.
22. Ibid.
23. Ibid.
24. Ibid.
25. Ibid.

Chapter 2
THE LANGUAGE OF EXCLUSION: CRACKING THE CODE

1. Ellen Langer, "Rethinking the Role of Thought in Social Interaction" in H. Harvey, W. Ickes, and R. Kidd, eds., *New Directions in Attribution Research,* vol. 2 (Hillsdale, NJ: Erlbaum, 1978), pp. 35–50.
2. Judy B. Rosener, "Ways Women Lead," *Harvard Business Review,* November–December 1990, p. 120.
3. Erving Goffman, *The Presentation of Self in Everyday Life* (Garden City, NY: Doubleday, 1959), p. 3.
4. Anne Huff, "Wives of the Organization," originally presented at the Women & Work Conference, Arlington, Texas, May 11, 1990.
5. Brian Dumaine, "America's Toughest Bosses," *Fortune,* October 8, 1993, p. 48.
6. Ibid.
7. "A Talk with Warren Bennis," *Psychology Today,* November–December 1993, pp. 30–31.
8. Sara Westendorf, "Getting the Guys on Your Side," *Working Woman,* July 1993, pp. 15–16.
9. Michael E. Porter, *Competitive Strategy* (New York: Free Press, 1980).
10. Fritz Heider, *The Psychology of Interpersonal Relations* (New York: John Wiley, 1958).
11. Frank Millar and Edna Rogers, "A Relational Approach to Interpersonal Communication," in Gerald R. Miller, ed., *Explorations in Interpersonal Communication* (Beverly Hills: Sage Publications, 1976). See also P. Watzlawick, J. Beavin, and D. D. Jackson, *Pragmatics of Human Communication* (New York, W. W. Norton, 1967).

Chapter 3
GETTING AT THE SUBTLE STUFF

1. "The New Old Boy," *Glamour,* February 1992, p. 197.
2. Anthony Mulac and James J. Bradac, "Women's Style in Problem Solving

Interactions: Powerless, or Simply Feminine?" in P. J. Kalbfleisch and M. J. Cody, eds., *Gender, Power, and Communication in Human Relationships* (Hillsdale, NJ: Erlbaum, 1995).

3. Irene H. Frieze, Jacquelynne E. Parsons, Paula B. Johnson, Diane N. Ruble, and Gail L. Zellman, *Women and Sex Roles: A Social Psychological Perspective* (New York: W. W. Norton, 1978).

4. Tony Lee, "Competition for Jobs Spawns Backstabbers and a Need for Armor," *Wall Street Journal*, 1993, p. B1.

5. Eugene J. Koprowski, "Cultural Myths: Clues to Effective Management," *Organizational Dynamics*, Autumn 1983, p. 43.

6. Ibid., p. 42.

7. Felice N. Schwartz, *Breaking with Tradition* (New York: Warner Books, 1992).

8. Daniel J. Canary and Brian H. Spitzberg, "Appropriateness and Effectiveness Perceptions of Conflict Strategies," *Human Communication Research*, Fall 1987.

9. Catalyst, "Women in Engineering: An Untapped Resource" (New York, 1992), p. 35.

10. Ibid., p. 24.

11. Catalyst, "On the Line" (New York, 1992), p. 28.

12. "As More Pregnant Women Work, Bias Complaints Rise," *Wall Street Journal*, December 6, 1993, p. B1.

13. Erving Goffman, *Interaction Ritual: Essays on Face-to-Face Behavior* (New York: Pantheon Books, 1967, 1982).

14. Susan Faludi, "Is Liberation Bad for Women?" *Washington Post Magazine*, October 20, 1991.

15. Felice N. Schwartz, "Management Women and the New Facts of Life," *Harvard Business Review*, January–February 1989.

16. Felice N. Schwartz, *Breaking with Tradition* (New York: Warner Books, 1992), pp. 148–149.

17. Ibid., p. 149.

18. "Stay-at-Home Moms Are Fashionable Again in Many Communities," *Wall Street Journal*, July 23, 1993, p. A1.

19. Ibid.

20. Ibid.

21. "We're Too Busy to Fight a 'Mommy War,' " Letters to the Editor, *Wall Street Journal*, August 23, 1993.

22. Susan Garland and Gail DeGeorge, "Can Hillary Put the Pieces Back Together?" *Business Week*, March 21, 1994, p. 40.

Chapter 4
STEREOTYPES VS. WORTHY DIFFERENCES

1. Arne Kalleberg and Kevin Leicht, "Gender and Organizational Performance: Determinants of Small Business Success," *Academy of Management Journal*, March 1991, p. 157.

2. Korn/Ferry International, "Decade of the Executive Woman" (New York, 1993).

3. O. C. Brenner, Joseph Tomkiewicz, and Virginia Ellen Schein, "The

Relationship Between Sex Role Stereotypes and Requisite Management Characteristics Revisited," *Academy of Management Journal,* no. 3, 1989, p. 668.

4. Louis Uchitell, "In Economics, a Subtle Exclusion," *New York Times,* January 11, 1993, p. C1.
5. Frederica Olivares, in "Ways Men and Women Lead," *Harvard Business Review,* January–February 1991, p. 151.
6. John Harwood and Geraldine Brooks, "Ms. President: Other Nations Elect Women to Lead Them, So Why Doesn't U.S.?" *Wall Street Journal,* December 14, 1993, p. A1.
7. Ann Morrison, *The New Leaders: Guidelines on Leadership Diversity in America* (San Francisco: Jossey-Bass, 1992), p. 4.
8. Rochelle Sharpe, "The Waiting Game: Women Make Strides, but Men Stay Firmly in Top Company Jobs," *Wall Street Journal,* March 29, 1994, p. A1.
9. Ibid.
10. Gail Fairhurst and William Sarr, "Confronting Illusory Participation in the 1980's," manuscript from Department of Communication, University of Cincinnati.
11. Jenifer S. Morrissey, "Why I Left," reprinted with permission.
12. Patricia O'Brien, "Why Men Don't Listen . . . and What It Costs Women at Work," *Working Woman,* February 1993, p. 56.
13. Catalyst, "Women in Engineering: An Untapped Resource" (New York, 1992).
14. Max DePree, *Leadership Is an Art* (New York: Doubleday, 1989).
15. Catalyst, "Women in Engineering," p. 4.
16. Erving Goffman, *Gender Advertisements* (New York: Harper & Row, 1976, 1979).
17. Ibid.
18. Arlie Russell Hochschild, "Gender Codes in Women's Advice Books" in Stephen H. Riggins, ed., *Beyond Goffman* (Berlin: Mouton de Gruyter, 1990).
19. Sonya Friedman, *Smart Cookies Don't Crumble* (New York: Pocket Books, 1985).
20. Robin Norwood, *Women Who Love Too Much: When You Keep Wishing and Hoping He'll Change* (Los Angeles: J. P. Tarcher, 1985).
21. Colette Dowling, *The Cinderella Complex* (New York: Summit Books, 1981).
22. Helgesen, Sally, *The Female Advantage* (New York: Doubleday, 1990).
23. Stephen H. Riggins, ed., *Beyond Goffman,* p. 292.
24. Mary Catherine Bateson, *Composing a Life* (New York: Plume, 1990), p. 214.

Chapter 5
LEADERSHIP: BY WHOSE STANDARDS?

1. Joe Flower, "A Conversation with Warren Bennis: The Chasm Between Management and Leadership," *Healthcare Forum Journal,* July–August 1990, pp. 58–62.
2. Peter M. Senge, *The Fifth Discipline: The Art and Practice of the Learning Organization* (New York: Doubleday, 1990).

3. Burt Nanus, *The Leader's Edge* (Chicago: Contemporary Books, 1989), p. 7.

4. Burt Nanus, *The Visionary Leader* (San Francisco: Jossey-Bass, 1992), p. 14.

5. Judy B. Rosener, "Ways Women Lead," *Harvard Business Review,* November–December, 1990.

6. Ibid., p. 122.

7. Nancy A. Nichols, "Whatever Happened to Rosie the Riveter?" *Harvard Business Review,* July–August 1993, pp. 57, 60.

8. Louis B. Barnes and Mark P. Kriger, "The Hidden Side of Organizational Leadership," *Sloan Management Review,* Fall 1986, p. 20.

9. Irene H. Frieze, Jacquelynne E. Parsons, Paula B. Johnson, Diane N. Ruble, and Gail L. Zellman, *Women and Sex Roles: A Social Psychological Perspective* (New York: W. W. Norton, 1978).

10. Ross Buck, *The Communication of Emotion* (New York: The Guilford Press, 1984).

11. Dennis K. Mumby and Linda L. Putnam, "The Politics of Emotion: A Feminist Reading of Bounded Rationality," *Academy of Management Review,* no. 3, 1992, pp. 465–486.

12. Arlie Russell Hochschild, "Gender Codes in Women's Advice Books" in Stephen H. Riggins, ed., *Beyond Goffman* (Berlin: Mouton de Gruyter, 1990).

13. Frieze et al., *Women and Sex Roles.*

14. Alice H. Eagly, Mona G. Makhijani, and Bruce G. Klonsky, "Gender and the Evaluation of Leaders: A Meta-Analysis," *Psychological Bulletin,* no. 1, 1992, pp. 3–22.

15. B. M. Bass and R. M. Stogdill, *Bass and Stogdill's Handbook of Leadership,* third ed. (New York: Free Press, 1990), pp. 726–727.

16. Terri R. Lituchy and Wendy J. Wiswall, "The Role of Masculine and Feminine Speech Patterns in Proposal Acceptance," *Management Communication Quarterly,* May 1991, pp. 450–465.

17. Patricia Hayes Andrews, "Gender Differences in Persuasive Communication and Attribution of Success and Failure," *Human Communication Research,* Spring 1987, pp. 372–385.

18. Deborah Tannen, "Wears Jump Suit. Sensible Shoes. Uses Husband's Last Name," *New York Times Magazine,* June 20, 1993, p. 18.

19. Ibid.

20. Anne Huff, "Wives of the Organization," paper originally presented at the Women and Work Conference, Arlington, Texas, May 11, 1990.

21. Peter Ferdinand Drucker, *The Effective Executive* (London: Pan Books, 1981).

Chapter 6
POWER PLAYS AND DISPLAYS

1. David McClelland, *Power: The Inner Experience* (New York: Irvington, Halsted Press, 1975).

2. B. M. Bass and R. M. Stogdill, *Handbook of Leadership* (New York: Free Press, 1981).

3. R. P. French Jr. and Bertram Raven, "The Bases of Social Power" in Dorwin Cartwright, ed., *Studies in Social Power* (Ann Arbor, MI: Institute for Social Research, 1959).

4. Irene H. Frieze, Jacquelynne E. Parsons, Paula B. Johnson, Diane N. Ruble, and Gail L. Zellman, *Women and Sex Roles: A Social Psychological Perspective* (New York: W. W. Norton, 1978).

5. Machiavelli, *The Prince* (Chicago: The Great Books Foundation, 1955), p. 55.

6. Ibid., p. 59.

7. "The New Power of Women Entrepreneurs," *Business Week,* April 18, 1994, p. 142. See also Wendy Zellner, Susan Chandler, Kevin Kelly, "Women Entrepreneurs: They're Forming Small Businesses at Twice the Rate of Men," *Business Week,* April 18, 1994, p. 104. See also Laurel Touby, "The New Bankrolls Behind Women's Businesses," *Business Week,* Sept. 21, 1992, p. 70.

8. Sun Tzu, *The Art of War,* edited and with a foreword by James Clavell (New York: Delta, 1983), p. 22.

9. Rosabeth Moss Kanter, *Men and Women of the Corporation* (New York: Basic Books, 1993).

10. John O'Neil, *The Paradox of Success* (New York: G. P. Putnam's Sons, 1993).

11. Pat Heim and Susan Golant, *Hardball for Women* (Los Angeles: Lowell House, 1992).

12. John O'Neil, *The Paradox of Success.*

13. Carol Gilligan, *In a Different Voice* (Cambridge, MA: Harvard University Press, 1992), p. 62.

14. Ibid.

15. Henry David Thoreau, *Walden* (Boston: Houghton Mifflin, 1964).

16. Warren Bennis, *The Invented Self* (Reading, MA: Addison-Wesley, 1993).

17. Jeffrey Pfeffer, *Managing with Power: Politics and Influence in Organizations* (Boston: Harvard Business School Press, 1992), p. 49.

18. "Reno, the Real Thing," *Time,* July 12, 1993.

19. Natasha Josefowitz, "Management Men and Women: Closed vs. Open Doors," *Harvard Business Review,* September–October 1980.

20. Robert B. Cialdini, *Influence* (New York: Quill, 1984).

21. Stephen Covey, *The Seven Habits of Highly Effective People: Restoring the Character Ethic* (New York: Simon and Schuster, 1989, 1990).

22. Deborah Tannen, *You Just Don't Understand* (New York: Ballantine Books, 1990).

23. Robert B. Cialdini, *Influence.*

24. Daniel J. Brass and Marlene E. Burkhardt, "Potential Power and Power Use: An Investigation of Structure and Behavior," *Academy of Management Journal,* June 1993, p. 444.

25. Ibid., p. 446.

Chapter 7
WHEN TO TALK, WHEN TO WALK

1. Michele Galen and Ann Therese Palmer, "White, Male and Worried," *Business Week,* January 31, 1994, pp. 50–55.

2. Dr. Keith Russell Abdow, *Washington Post,* December 10, 1991.

3. Nancy Dodd McCann and Thomas A. McGinn, *Harassed* (Homewood, IL: Business One Irwin, 1992).

4. E. P. Hollander, "Conformity, Stature and Idiosyncrasy Credit," *Psychological Review* 65, 1958, pp. 117–127.

5. "Woman Who First Reported Tailhook Sex Scandal Resigns," *Los Angeles Times,* February 11, 1994, p. A18.

6. Alan J. Rowe, *Managing with Style: A Guide to Understanding, Assessing, and Improving Decision Making* (San Francisco: Jossey-Bass, 1987).

7. Klaus Fielder, Gun R. Semin, and Catrin Finkenauer, "The Battle of Words Between Gender Groups," *Human Communication Research,* vol. 19, no. 3, 1993, pp. 409–441.

8. Myra and David Sadker, *Failing at Fairness* (New York: Charles Scribner's Sons, 1994).

9. Carolyn G. Heilbrun, *Writing a Woman's Life* (New York: Ballantine Books, 1988).

10. E. E. Maccoby, "Differential Socialization of Boys and Girls," paper presented at the meeting of the American Psychological Association, Hawaii, 1972.

11. M. S. Horner, "Toward an Understanding of Achievement-Related Conflicts in Women," *Journal of Social Issues,* no. 2, 1972, pp. 157–175.

12. Rosabeth Moss Kanter, *Men and Women of the Corporation* (New York: Basic Books, 1993).

13. Ibid.

Chapter 8
ET TU, BRUTE?

1. Pamela Kruger, "What Women Think of Women Bosses," *Working Woman,* June 1993, pp. 40–43, 80–85.

2. Cornell study, quote from Dr. Timothy Judge, *Wall Street Journal,* March 8, 1994.

3. Marilyn Loden, *Feminine Leadership* (New York: Random House, 1985).

4. Dawn-Marie Driscoll and Carol R. Goldberg, *Members of the Club* (New York: Free Press, 1993).

5. Karlene H. Roberts, "Communicating in Organizations" in J. E. Rosenzweig and F. E. Kast, ed., *Modules in Management* (Science Research Associates, 1984).

6. M. Granovetter, "The Strength of Weak Ties," *American Journal of Sociology,* May 1973, pp. 1360–1380.

7. "Women Make Strides but Men Stay Firmly in Top Company Jobs," *Wall Street Journal,* March 29, 1994, p. A8.

8. Ibid.

9. Ibid.

Chapter 9
CHOOSING THE RIGHT WORK CLIMATE

1. Gail Fairhurst, "The Communication Between Leaders and Their Followers: A

Review and Commentary" in K. Jablin and L. Putnam, eds., *The New Handbook in Organizational Communication* (in press, 1995).

2. Gretchen Spreitzer, paper presented at the 1994 Academy of Management Annual Meeting, Dallas, Texas.

3. Peter Drucker, speech given at the Leadership Institute inaugural symposium, Pasadena, California, April 2, 1992.

4. Marilyn Ferguson, *The Aquarian Conspiracy: Personal and Social Transformation in Our Time* (New York: Tarcher/Perigee, 1987).

5. Emmeline dePillis, Michael Driver, Jay Mahoney, and Karen Gang, "MBA Sex Differences in Leadership Qualities," paper presented at the 1994 Academy of Management Annual Meeting, Dallas, Texas.